The Famous Five and You
Find Adventure!

2

Join the Famous Five on their surprise
adventure at Kirrin Cottage. You might
discover a map to a 'secret way' or track
down some mystery thieves. *You* can
choose a pathway for the Five to reveal the
crooks – but will you go straight to them or
will you take a false trail along the way?

This exciting game story is based on Enid
Blyton's *Five Go Adventuring Again*.

Join the action in
The Famous Five and You!

Enid Blyton, who died in 1968 at the age of 71 became, during her lifetime, Britain's best-loved and most popular author, and is still considered to have wielded a greater influence than any other author over children's writing in the post-war years. She loved young people, and wrote for 'all children, any children, everywhere' – over 600 books, many songs, poems and plays.

THE FAMOUS FIVE ② & YOU

FIND ADVENTURE!

An Enid Blyton story
devised and adapted
by Mary Danby

Based on Enid Blyton's
Five Go Adventuring Again

Illustrated by Trevor Parkin

KNIGHT BOOKS
Hodder and Stoughton

*First published in Great Britain in
1987 by Knight Books*

Enid Blyton is a Trade Mark of
Darrell Waters Limited

British Library C.I.P.

Danby, Mary
    Find adventure! – (The Famous
five and you; 2).
    1. Adventure games – Juvenile
literature
I. Title   II. Parkin, Trevor
III. Blyton, Enid. Five go
adventuring again
IV. Series
793'.9   GV1203

ISBN 0-340-41101-5

Printed and bound in Great Britain
for Hodder and Stoughton
Paperbacks, a division of Hodder
and Stoughton Limited, Mill Road,
Dunton Green, Sevenoaks, Kent.
TN13 2YA. (Editorial Office:
47 Bedford Square, London
WC1B 3DP) by Cox & Wyman
Limited, Reading, Berks. Photoset by
Rowland Phototypesetting Limited,
Bury St Edmunds, Suffolk

THE FAMOUS FIVE – AND YOU

Unlike an ordinary book, which you can read straight through from beginning to end, this is a gamebook, in which *you* choose how the story should go.

Begin at paragraph number 1. At the end of each paragraph you are told which paragraph to read next. Sometimes you will find you have a choice. (For instance, at the end of paragraph 10 you have to decide which platform the train will leave from.)

Every time you have a choice to make, there will be one way that is the quickest and best – and you have to guess (or work out, if you can) which it is. If you choose the wrong paragraph, you can still carry on reading, but when you find yourself back at the main story you will find you have picked up a few 'red herrings'.

A red herring is the name given to something that carries you away from the main subject (as when someone is telling you a story and puts in all sorts of details that don't really matter). Your aim is to try and stay on the main track, without going off down the little side roads.

See if you can make the right choices and find your way to the end of the story without picking up too many red herrings. Red herrings are represented in the text by a symbol: (Use a pencil and paper to add up your score as you go along.) Then turn to the back of the book to see how well The Famous Five (and You) have done.

1

It was the last week of the Christmas term, and the girls at Graylands school were looking forward to the Christmas holidays. Anne sat down at the breakfast table and picked up a letter addressed to her.

'Hello, look at this!' she said to her cousin Georgina. 'A letter from Daddy, and I had one only the other day.'

'I hope it's not bad news,' said George. She was quite a tomboy and wouldn't allow anyone to call her Georgina – even the teachers called her George. She looked anxiously at Anne as her cousin read the letter.

'Oh George – we can't go home for the holidays!' said Anne with tears in her eyes. 'Mummy's got chicken pox and Daddy's in quarantine for it, so they can't have us back. Isn't it just too bad?'

Go to **7**.

2

If you have arrived from **21**, *score one red herring:* 🐟.

'Well!' said Uncle Quentin as they sat around the tea-table. 'I hear I've got to get a tutor for you! At least, for the two boys. My word, you *will* have to behave yourself with a tutor, I can tell you!'

This was meant to be a joke, but it didn't sound very nice to Anne and George. People you had to behave well with were usually very strict and tiresome. Both girls were glad when George's father had gone back to his study.

Later, when George and Anne were tucked up in bed in their familiar old room, Timmy curled himself up happily in his basket by the window seat.

'The boys will be back tomorrow,' said Anne as she cuddled down under the blankets. 'It'll be super seeing them again!'

Go to **6**.

3

George flopped down in a corner of the carriage, and Timmy curled up at her feet. Anne put the small case she was carrying on to the rack and then sat down. There was no point trying to coax George out of her sulks yet. Anne would just have to wait until George was feeling better. Maybe the thought of going home for the holidays would cheer her up quickly.

Just then the ticket collector came into their compartment. 'Tickets, please, young ladies!' he said.

Anne and George handed him their tickets for Kirrin.

He looked at them closely. 'My goodness!' he exclaimed. 'You're on the wrong train! Quickly, now, get over to platform six. The train leaves in three minutes!'

Go to **13**.

4

Aunt Fanny smiled. 'Your uncle bought a new car quite recently,' she said, 'and I expect Timmy's puzzled because he doesn't recognise the sound of the engine.'

'A new car!' exclaimed Dick in excitement. 'What kind is it?'

Just then the back door opened and George's father came in.

Go to **12**.

5

If you have arrived from **13***, score two red herrings :* ⌒⌒ .

'It will be lovely to go across to Kirrin Island again, George,' said Anne as the train raced along.

'We shan't be able to,' said George. 'The sea is terribly rough around the island in the winter. It would be too dangerous to try to row there.'

'Oh, what a pity!' said Anne, disappointed. 'I was looking forward to some more adventures there.'

It was a long time before the train reached the little station that served Kirrin, but at last it stopped at the tiny platform.

'I wonder if my father has come to meet us,' said George.

Anne looked out of the window. She saw a young woman with two small children, but she couldn't see Uncle Quentin anywhere.

Has Uncle Quentin come to meet them? If you think he has, go to 17. If not, go to 22.

6

The next day the boys arrived. Anne and George went to meet them with Timmy. George drove the pony and trap with Timmy beside her. Anne could hardly wait for the train to stop at the station. She ran along the platform, looking for Julian and Dick in the carriages that passed.

Then she saw them. They were looking out of a window at the back of the train, waving and yelling.

'Anne! Anne! Here we are! Hello, George! Oh, there's Timmy!'

Julian and Dick tumbled out of the train, and the four children stood chattering excitedly while Timmy bounced around their legs, thrilled to see the boys again.

The porter heaved the trunks into the trap, and the four of them began to climb in.

'Do you . . . do you think I could have a go at driving?' asked Anne.

If you think George should let Anne drive the trap, go to **11**.
If not, go to **15**.

7

'Oh, I *am* sorry,' said George.

'Whatever will the two boys say?' said Anne, thinking of Julian and Dick, her brothers. 'They won't be able to go home either.'

'Well, what are you going to do for the holidays, then?' asked George.

Anne read a few more lines of the letter and then

gave a delighted exclamation: 'George! We're to come to you at Kirrin Cottage again – but oh, blow, blow, blow! We've got to have a tutor for the holidays. Julian and Dick have been ill with flu twice this term and have got bchind in their work.'

'A tutor! How sickening! That means I'll have to do lessons too, I'll bet!' said George gloomily. 'When my mother and father see my report they'll find out how little I know. What horrid hols they'll be!'

Go to **10**.

8

'I'm working very hard on a book,' explained Uncle Quentin. 'I've been working out a secret theory – a secret idea – and when it's all finished I'm going to take it to someone in the government and my idea will be used for the good of the country.'

'That sounds exciting,' said Anne.

'I'll need lots of peace and quiet,' Uncle Quentin went on. 'So you children will have to behave yourselves.'

George and Anne looked at each other in dismay. Between having to have a tutor and having to keep quiet because Uncle Quentin was working, it looked like being a pretty dull holiday!

Go to **21**.

9

If you have arrived from **23**, *score* ◯◁ ◯◁.

Soon they all arrived at Kirrin Cottage. The boys were really pleased to see their aunt, and rather relieved when she said their uncle wasn't at home.

'He's gone to interview two or three men who answered the advertisement for a tutor,' she said. 'He'll be back soon. Now up you all go and wash your hands before tea.'

Aunt Fanny had made a lovely lot of buns and a great big cake for tea, and soon there was not much left of either!

Just as they were finishing tea Timmy suddenly started to bark, and all the hair on the back of his neck stood up.

'What is it, Timmy?' asked George. 'Is Father back? Or is there someone else outside?'

If you think it is Uncle Quentin, go to **4**. *If you think it might be a stranger, go to* **20**.

10

The end of term came quickly. Anne and George packed up their trunks and put on the labels, enjoying the noise and excitement of the last two days. The big school coaches rolled up to the door and the girls clambered in.

'Off to Kirrin again!' said Anne. 'Come on,

Timmy darling, you can sit between me and George.'

Graylands school allowed the girls to keep their pets, and Timmy, George's big mongrel dog, had been a great success in his first term there. He had behaved extremely well.

It wasn't very long before they reached the station in London where they were to catch the train for Kirrin.

'Come on,' said George. 'The Kirrin train always goes from platform six.'

'Oh no, George,' said Miss Johnson, one of the teachers. 'Your train goes from platform eight.'

If you think they should head for platform six, go to **14**. *If you think they should head for platform eight, go to* **19**.

11

George hesitated. 'It's not as easy as it looks, you know,' she said.

'Oh please let me try,' begged Anne. 'If you sit beside me you can tell me what to do.'

'All right, then,' said George, 'but you must do exactly what I tell you.'

They all climbed into the trap, and Anne picked up the reins. She guided the pony carefully out of the station yard, and soon they were bowling down the road towards Kirrin Cottage. The sea sparkled in the winter sun, and they could see Kirrin Island looking much nearer than it really was.

'What a pity we shan't be able to go over there,' said Dick.

'Never mind, I'm sure we'll be able to find lots of other things to do – and it will soon be Christmas,' said George happily.

Go to **18**.

12

If you have arrived from **28**, *score* ◯.

Uncle Quentin shook hands with the two boys and asked them if they had had a good term.

'Did you get a tutor, Uncle Quentin?' asked Anne, who could see that everyone was simply bursting to know this.

'Ah – yes, I did,' said her uncle. 'I interviewed three applicants, and had almost chosen the last one when another fellow came in, all in a hurry. Said he had only just seen the advertisement, and hoped he wasn't too late.'

'Did you choose him?' asked Dick.

'I did,' said his uncle. 'He seemed a most intelligent fellow. A good bit older than the others. Even knew about me and my work! He'll fit in here very well. It will be nice to have him to talk to sometimes in the evenings.'

The children couldn't help feeling that the new tutor sounded rather alarming.

Go to **27**.

Anne grabbed her case from the rack and she, George and Timmy scrambled out of the carriage and rushed down the platform, across the station, and up to platform six. The guard was just about to blow his whistle as they came flying up the platform.

'Quickly, now,' called the guard. 'In you get! The train's just leaving.'

The two girls and Timmy clambered into the train just in time, and collapsed breathlessly into a compartment.

'Whew!' said Anne. 'That was a near thing!'

The guard blew his whistle and the train sped off westwards.

Go to **5**.

'But Miss Johnson, the Kirrin train always leaves from platform six,' said George. 'Look!' She pointed at the big departures board.

'Oh yes,' said the teacher. 'You're quite right, George. Off you go, then. Have a good holiday, won't you?'

'Thanks very much, Miss Johnson,' chorused the girls, and they set off down the platform, Timmy trotting at George's heels.

They settled themselves in a compartment, and

before long the guard blew his whistle and the train sped out of the station towards the west.

Go to **5**.

15

'No,' said George, 'I'm afraid not. It isn't as easy as it looks, and you could have a nasty accident if something went wrong.'

George took the reins, and soon the pony was going along the road at a spanking trot.

'It's good that Mummy is getting on all right, isn't it?' said Dick. 'I was disappointed not to go home, but still, it will be good to be back at Kirrin Cottage again. I wish we could have some more exciting adventures.'

'There's one snag about these holidays,' said Julian, 'and that's the tutor. I hear we've got to have one because Dick and I missed so much school this term. I wonder what he'll be like.'

Go to **9**.

16

'Children!' called Aunt Fanny. 'Come down here, please!'

The children ran downstairs to the kitchen.

'I'm very sorry,' said Aunt Fanny, 'but I'm

afraid you won't be able to go Christmas shopping after all.'

'Oh Aunt Fanny!' wailed Anne. 'I was looking forward to it so much!'

'Your father can't go to meet Mr Roland tomorrow,' explained their aunt. 'He's just had a telephone call from someone very important – to do with his secret theory – and he'll have to go and see this person tomorrow morning.'

'But couldn't you go to meet the tutor, Mother?' asked George.

Go to **29**.

17

As the girls jumped off the train, Uncle Quentin appeared on the platform. Aunt Fanny was with him.

'Hello, George, darling. Hello, Anne!' said George's mother. 'Anne, I'm so sorry about your mother, but she's getting on all right, you'll be glad to know.'

'Oh good!' said Anne. 'It's nice of you to have us, Aunt Fanny.'

Uncle Quentin had been saying hello to Timmy, who was gambolling around in great excitement. He looked at the two girls sternly. 'I hope you four children aren't going to be a nuisance this holidays,' he said.

Go to **8**.

The pony went *clip-clopping* along the road. Anne was managing the reins quite well, though once or twice George put her hand over Anne's to help her.

'You're doing a really good job of driving the pony, Anne,' said Julian. 'Perhaps George could give you lessons during the hols.'

'That would be super,' said Anne, her eyes shining. She was very fond of animals, and would have really loved to have a pony of her own. But as they lived in a town, she had nowhere to keep it.

'We'll be able to see Kirrin Cottage after we go around this bend,' said George. 'I expect Mother will . . .'

But just then a cat shot out of the hedge by the side of the road, straight under the pony's hooves!

Go to **23**.

19

'But Miss Johnson, the Kirrin train *always* leave from platform six,' said George.

'Don't argue, George dear,' said the teacher. 'Just go along to platform eight and get yourselves and Timmy into the train.'

George set off for platform eight looking sulky. She was sure that it was the wrong platform!

'Come on, Anne,' she called over her shoulder. 'Can't you walk any faster?'

Poor Anne struggled to keep up with George as she stamped off across the station. It was a jolly bad start to the holidays to have George in a sulk already!

They reached platform eight and climbed into the train.

Go to **3**.

20

Timmy ran to the back door and stood swishing his tail and barking furiously.

Aunt Fanny got up. 'I'll go and see who it is,' she said. 'I'm sure Timmy wouldn't bark like that if it was your uncle.'

She opened the back door and Timmy flew out, growling fiercely.

'Timmy, Timmy, come here!' called George, getting up from the table and going to the back door. 'Who is it, Mother?'

Go to **28**.

21

They piled the trunks into the back of the pony trap and were soon back at the pretty old cottage that belonged to George's parents. When Uncle Quentin had helped to unload the trunks, he went straight into his study.

The girls ran upstairs to wash their hands before tea.

'I'm simply starving!' said Anne as they came downstairs again. 'I hope there's plenty to eat.'

Aunt Fanny told the girls to sit down, and called George's father.

'Quentin, tea's ready!'

Go to **2**.

22

As the girls jumped off the train, George's mother appeared on the platform.

'Hello, George, darling. Hello, Anne!' she said, and gave both of them a hug. 'Anne, I'm so sorry about your mother, but she's getting on all right, you'll be glad to know.'

'Oh good!' said Anne. 'It's nice of you to have us, Aunt Fanny. We'll try to be good!'

'How is Father?' asked George. 'Is he still working hard?'

George's father was a scientist, a very clever man, but rather frightening. He had little patience with children, and the four of them had felt very much afraid of him at times during the summer.

'Oh, he's still working very hard on his book,' said Aunt Fanny. 'You know, he's been working out a secret theory – a secret idea – and putting it all into his book. He says that once it's all finished he's going to take it to someone in the government, and then his idea will be used for the good of the country.'

Go to **26**.

23

The pony swerved sharply, and the reins were pulled out of Anne's hands! George made a desperate grab at them and just managed to catch hold of the slippery leather. It took her a moment or two to get the pony under control again. Soon, however, he had calmed down, and George brought him to a halt.

'Move over, Anne,' she said. 'I think I'd better drive the rest of the way home.'

Anne did as George said, secretly relieved. It had given her a nasty fright when the pony shied, and she was feeling rather shaky!

George picked up the reins again, clicked her tongue, and off they went, their voices ringing in the frosty air.

Go to **9**.

24

'Well, all right, then,' said Uncle Quentin. 'I suppose I could go and meet Mr Roland.'

'I hope he won't be too strict,' said Dick, later that evening. 'It'll spoil the holidays if we have someone down on us all the time. And I do hope he'll like Timmy.'

'Like Timmy!' exclaimed George. 'Of course he'll like Timmy! How couldn't he?'

'Well, there *are* people who don't like dogs, you know, George,' replied Dick.

Just then they heard Aunt Fanny calling from downstairs.

Go to **16**.

25

If you have arrived from **29**, *score* ⌇ ⌇.

Next morning they got the trap and set off down the lanes to the station.

'Did all this land belong to your family once upon a time?' asked Julian.

'Yes, all of it,' said George. 'Now we don't own anything except Kirrin Island, our own house and that farm away over there – Kirrin Farm.' She pointed with her whip. The children saw an old farmhouse standing on a hill a good way off.

'Who lives there?' asked Julian.

'Oh, an old farmer and his wife,' said George. 'They're very nice. We'll go over there one day if you like. Sometimes in the summertime they take people who want a holiday.'

A moment later George swung the trap into the station yard. The train was just pulling in.

Go to **33**.

'Oh Aunt Fanny, it does sound exciting!' said
Anne. 'What's the secret?'

'I can't tell you that, silly girl,' said her aunt,
laughing. 'Why, I don't know it myself!'

The girls put their trunks in the back of the trap
and they were soon bowling along the frosty roads
to Kirrin Cottage.

'Good old Kirrin Cottage!' said Anne as they
came in sight of the pretty old house.

The girls went into the house.

'Quentin! Quentin!' called George's mother.
'The girls are here!'

Uncle Quentin came out of his study. Anne
thought he looked taller and darker than ever.
'And frownier!' she said to herself as she greeted
him.

'Time for tea,' said Aunt Fanny.

Go to **2**.

Uncle Quentin smiled at their gloomy faces.
'You'll like Mr Roland,' he said. 'He knows how to
handle youngsters – knows he's got to be very firm,
and to see that you know a good bit more at the end
of the holidays than you did at the beginning.'

'When is he coming?' asked George.

'Tomorrow,' said her father. 'You can all go to

meet him at the station. He's arriving on the ten-thirty train.'

'Oh . . .' said Anne, looking disappointed.

Uncle Quentin raised an eyebrow.

'We *had* thought of going Christmas shopping tomorrow morning,' explained Julian.

'Oh please, Father, couldn't you meet the tutor while we go shopping?' pleaded George.

If you think Uncle Quentin agrees to meet the tutor, go to **24**. *If not, go to* **30**.

28

In the back yard stood a small dark man, rather shabbily dressed and carrying a large case that he was trying to open. Timmy stood by, growling softly.

'Can I help you?' asked Aunt Fanny.

'I wondered if I could interest you in buying any of my dusters, pegs or brushes,' said the man. 'I've got an excellent selection here.'

As he spoke, his eyes darted past Aunt Fanny, trying to see into the house.

'I don't think so,' said Aunt Fanny. 'I'm afraid I never buy at the door. Good day to you.'

She shut the door and went back to the table with George.

'I didn't like the look of that man,' George said to the others. 'I don't think Timmy did, either!'

They were in the middle of clearing away the tea

things when the back door opened and George's father came in.

Go to **12**.

29

'No,' said Aunt Fanny, 'I've got a great deal to do tomorrow. I've got to get Mr Roland's room ready and do some baking for the weekend.'

'As far as I'm concerned Mr Roland can jolly well sleep in the outhouse,' muttered George. Fortunately her mother didn't hear her!

'So you children can take the pony and trap and meet him at the station,' her mother went on. 'It will be a good chance for you to get to know him.'

The children went back upstairs feeling rather disappointed. They had all been looking forward to going to the town and seeing all the Christmas decorations, and buying presents for each other.

'Never mind!' said Julian as they went to bed. 'We'll go another day.'

Go to **25**.

30

'Oh no,' said Uncle Quentin. 'You must certainly go to meet Mr Roland. I told him you would. And mind, you four – no nonsense with him!'

'I hope he won't be too strict,' said Dick later

that evening. 'It'll spoil the holidays if we have someone down on us all the time. And I do hope he'll like Timmy.'

'Like Timmy!' exclaimed George. 'Of course he'll like Timmy! How couldn't he?'

'Well, there *are* people who don't like dogs, you know, George,' replied Dick.

'If Mr Roland doesn't like Timmy, I'll not do a single thing for him,' said George fiercely. 'Not one single thing!'

Go to **25**.

31

If you have arrived from **48**, *score* ⌒⊲.

'Yes. George and Anne are outside in the trap,' said Julian.

'George and Anne?' said Mr Roland in a puzzled voice. 'I thought the others were girls. I didn't know there was a third boy.'

'Oh George is a girl,' said Dick with a laugh. 'She won't answer if she's called Georgina. You'd better call her George, Mr Roland!'

'Really?' said Mr Roland in a rather chilly tone.

'Timmy's out there, too,' said Dick.

'Oh – and is Timmy a boy or a girl?' enquired Mr Roland cautiously.

'A dog!' said Dick, grinning.

Go to **36**.

'Well,' he said, 'I don't think I want to shake hands with Timmy anyway.'

'It's all right,' said George, frowning at him. 'Timmy won't hurt you.'

'I'm sure you're right, Georgina,' said Mr Roland mildly. 'It's just that I think it's rather silly to make animals behave like humans.'

George scowled at him. She was cross with him because he had called her Georgina – and even crosser because he had been rude about Timmy!

Go to **46**.

33

Not many people got off. A woman clambered out with a basket. A young man, the son of the village baker, leapt out, followed by an older man in a felt hat, who climbed down slowly. He was very tall and thin, and carried a big black umbrella hooked over one arm.

'Do you think that's him?' Dick asked Julian. 'Uncle Quentin said he was an older person.'

Then right at the end of the train rather an odd-looking man got out. He was short and burly, with a beard like a sailor's. His eyes were piercingly blue, and his thick hair was sprinkled with grey. He glanced up and down the platform, and then beckoned to a porter.

'Maybe that's him,' said Julian. 'It looks as if we'll have to ask.'

Which one is Mr Roland? If you think he's the man in the felt hat, go to 44. If you think he's the man with the beard, go to 39.

34

Mr Roland was shown up to his room when he arrived. Aunt Fanny came down and spoke to the children. 'Well, he seems very nice – youngish and jolly.'

'Aunt Fanny, we shan't begin lessons until after Christmas, shall we?' asked Julian anxiously.

'Of course you will!' said his aunt. 'It's almost a week to Christmas – you don't suppose we've asked Mr Roland to come and do nothing until Christmas is over, do you?'

The children groaned.

'You won't begin lessons until tomorrow, though,' said Aunt Fanny. 'Why don't you go for a walk? It's a lovely morning.'

'Let's go over to Kirrin Farm,' Julian suggested.

'Right!' said George. She whistled to Timmy.

They set off along the lane behind the house, and then on to a path over the common. After a short while they came to a place where the path divided.

'Which path do we take, George?' asked Dick. 'Left or right?'

'Well, actually, they both lead to the farm,' said George.

If you think they should turn right, go to **38**. *If you think they should turn left, go to* **43**.

35

Dick loved gingerbread. It was really his favourite cake, and his mother always sent him back to school at the beginning of term with a big tin of gingerbread in his trunk. Dick always meant to make it last a long time, but he usually ate it all within the first two or three weeks of term.

'Could I have a cup of tea, love?' asked Mr Sanders, coming in from the farmyard.

'I'll put the kettle on just as soon as I've given the children something to eat,' replied his wife.

Go to **54**.

36

Mr Roland seemed rather taken aback.

'A dog?' he said. 'I didn't know there was a dog in the household. Your uncle said nothing to me about a dog.'

'Don't you like dogs?' asked Julian in surprise.

'No,' said Mr Roland shortly, 'but I dare say your dog won't worry me much. Hello, hello – so here are the girls! How do you do?'

George wasn't very pleased at being called a girl. She always tried to be a boy. She held out her hand to Mr Roland and said nothing. Anne smiled at him, and Mr Roland thought she was much the nicer of the two.

'Timmy! Shake hands with Mr Roland!' said Julian. This was one of Timmy's really good tricks. Mr Roland looked down at the big dog; Tim looked back at him.

*If you think Timmy obeys Julian, go to **45**. If not, go to **40**.*

37

*If you have arrived from **47**, score ⌀.*

George talked soothingly to Timmy as she worked to release him. 'There now, Timmy,' she said. 'I'll soon have you free, poor old thing.'

'Is he all right?' gasped Anne, who was out of breath.

'Oh yes,' said George. 'He'll be fine as soon as I get this wire off his collar.'

A moment later Timmy was free. He went bounding around them, wagging his tail and licking George's hand as if to say thank you.

The children went on with their walk, and before long they had reached Kirrin Farm, which was a lovely old house built of white stone. George opened the gate and they went into the farmyard.

*Go to **50**.*

'Which is the quickest way?' asked Anne.

'The right-hand path,' said George. 'Come on!'

It was lovely walking in the December sun. Their feet rang on the frosty path, and Timmy's blunt claws made quite a noise as he pattered up and down.

After a good long walk across the common the children came to the farmhouse. It was built of white stone. George opened the gate and they went into the farmyard.

Go to **50**.

39

Julian and Dick went up to the bearded man.

'Are you Mr Roland?' they asked.

'I am,' said the man. 'I suppose you are Julian and Dick?'

'That's right,' said the boys together. 'We brought the pony and trap for your luggage.'

'Oh fine,' said Mr Roland. His bright blue eyes looked the boys up and down, and he smiled. Julian and Dick liked him. He seemed sensible and jolly.

'Are the other two here as well?' asked Mr Roland as they walked down the platform.

Go to **31**.

Very slowly and deliberately, Timmy turned his back on Mr Roland and climbed up into the trap! Usually he put out his paw at once when told to, and the children stared at him in amazement.

'Timmy! What's come over you?' cried Dick. Timmy put his ears down and didn't move.

'He doesn't like you', said George, looking at Mr Roland. 'That's very odd. He usually likes people. But perhaps it's because you don't like dogs.'

'You may be right,' said Mr Roland. 'I was very badly bitten once when I was a boy, and I've never really liked dogs since. But I dare say your Timmy will take to me sooner or later.'

Go to **46**.

Go to **46**.

41

Dick and George hadn't gone very far when George suddenly stopped. 'Listen!' she said. 'I thought I heard a noise.'

Dick listened carefully, but at first he couldn't hear anything. Then suddenly he heard a funny whimpering noise.

'That's Timmy!' said George. 'Come on, we must find him!'

They ran on down the path, and as they came around a curve there was poor Timmy caught under a fence by a piece of wire that had got twisted around his collar.

'Oh Timmy,' said George. 'Thank goodness I've found you!'

'I'll call the others,' said Dick. He shouted as loudly as he could: 'Anne! Julian! Come here quickly!'

It wasn't long before the other two came running around the curve to find them.

Go to **37**.

42

'These are my cousins,' said George, introducing the other three.

'I'm very pleased to meet you,' said Mrs

Sanders. 'Now, what would you like to drink? Hot milk? Cocoa?'

The children all chose cocoa, and Mrs Sanders put a pan of milk on the stove. In a little while there were four steaming mugs on the big scrubbed kitchen table, and Mrs Sanders was fetching a big round tin from the pantry.

'What do you think I've got in here?' she asked, smiling.

'Shortbread!' said Anne.

'Gingerbread!' guessed Dick.

If you think Anne is right, go to **54**. *If you think Dick is right, go to* **35**.

43

'Let's turn left,' said Dick. 'Come on!'

It was lovely walking in the December sun. Their feet rang on the frosty path, and Timmy's blunt claws made quite a noise as he pattered up and down.

'Are you sure we're going the right way, George?' asked Julian. 'We don't seem to be heading towards the farmhouse.'

'This path winds around quite a lot,' said George. 'There are one or two marshy places on this common, and if you go off the path you can easily stumble into one of them. It's better to stick to the path, even though it isn't so direct.'

Just then a man came in sight, walking along the path towards them.

Go to **49**.

44

The man in the felt hat walked down the platform towards the guard's van, then spoke to the guard. Julian and Dick were still hesitating over which of the men to approach. As they watched, the guard lifted a bicycle out of the van and the man in the felt hat started to wheel it down the platform.

'Well, Uncle Quentin never said anything about Mr Roland bringing a bicycle,' said Julian, 'so that can't be him.'

'Mr Roland might not have told Uncle Quentin about the bicycle,' argued Dick. 'I'm sure that's him. Let's go and ask.'

Go to **48**.

45

'Come on, Timmy, shake hands!' repeated Julian.

Timmy went on staring at Mr Roland. Julian was puzzled. Usually Timmy was very obedient and loved showing how clever he was, but for some reason he didn't want to shake hands with Mr Roland.

'Shake hands, Timmy!' said Julian for the third time, and this time Timmy very slowly raised one of his paws and held it out to Mr Roland. But much to the children's surprise, as Timmy did so he gave a long, low growl.

Mr Roland, who had stepped forward to take Timmy's paw, jumped back in alarm.

Go to **32**.

46

If you have arrived from **32**, *score* ◯◁.

They all got into the trap. It was rather a tight squeeze. Timmy looked at Mr Roland's ankles as if he would like to nibble them, which made Anne want to laugh.

Mr Roland joked with the boys as they drove along, and they both began to feel that Uncle Quentin hadn't made such a bad choice after all. Anne decided that she liked him, too. He had such a nice smile.

Only George said nothing. She sensed that the tutor disliked Timmy, and George wasn't prepared to like anyone who didn't take to Timmy at first sight.

Go to **34**.

47

They hurried off in the direction of Dick's voice and eventually came across Dick and George crouched down beside an old wire fence with Timmy between them. His collar was caught in the wire and he couldn't move.

Go to **37**.

48

But as the two boys started to walk towards the man in the felt hat, he got on his bicycle and rode away.

'Well,' said Dick, 'he certainly wasn't Mr Roland! It must be the man with the beard.'

They went up to the bearded man.

'Are you Mr Roland?' asked Dick.

'I am,' said the man. 'I suppose you two are Julian and Dick?'

'That's right,' said the boys together. 'We've brought the pony and trap for your luggage.'

'Oh good,' said Mr Roland. His bright blue eyes looked the boys up and down, and he smiled. Julian and Dick liked him. He seemed sensible and jolly.

'Are the other two here as well?' asked Mr Roland as they walked along the platform.

Go to **31**.

49

He was small and dark-haired with sallow skin, and he was carrying a large suitcase. The children had been walking side by side along the path, but they moved into single file to let the man go past them. He hurried by, not looking at them.

'Good morning,' said George politely, but the man didn't reply. He just walked rapidly along the path towards Kirrin.

'You know,' said George, 'I've seen that man somewhere before. I'm sure I have.' She frowned. 'I wonder who he is?'

They walked on, Timmy running to and fro and wagging his tail.

'Look at Timmy. I think he can smell rabbits,' said Anne. 'Do you remember how he chased them when we were on Kirrin Island last summer?'

'He never managed to catch one, did he?' replied Julian. 'Are there rabbits on this common, George?'

'Oh yes,' said George, 'lots of them, I think. There are masses of burrows, but you don't often see rabbits coming out of them. There are too many people about.'

But just then, to the children's surprise, a rabbit suddenly appeared on the path in front of them! Timmy gave it one startled look, and rushed up to it. The rabbit hopped away as fast as it could, with Timmy in pursuit.

Go **53**.

50

If you have arrived from **37**, *score* ⌒ ⌒ ⌒ ⌒.

Someone clattered around the nearby barn. It was an old man. George hailed him loudly: 'Hello, Mr Sanders! How are you?'

'Why, if it isn't George!' said Mr Sanders with a grin.

'These are my cousins,' shouted George. She turned to the others. 'He's deaf,' she said. 'You'll have to shout to make yourselves heard.'

'Come along inside and meet the wife,' said Mr Sanders. 'She'll be rare pleased to see you all.'

They went into the big farmhouse kitchen, where Mrs Sanders was bustling about. She was a small, lively old woman with grey hair and twinkling dark eyes.

'Well, George,' she said. 'It's nice to see you. Home for the holidays, I suppose?'

Go to **42**.

51

Timmy took no notice of George's stern shout. He flew out of the kitchen after the cat into the panelled hall. The cat tried to leap on top of an old grandfather clock, and, with a joyous bark, Timmy sprang too. He flung himself against a polished panel – and then a most extraordinary thing happened!

The panel disappeared.

George, who had followed Timmy out into the hall, gave a loud cry of surprise.

'Look! Come and look!'

Go to **63**.

52

Julian had a good look, but there didn't seem to be anything to see. It was all darkness behind, and stone wall. There certainly wasn't any treasure. He gave the torch to Dick, and then each of the children had a turn at peeping. Mrs Sanders had gone back to the kitchen. She was used to the sliding panel!

'She said this house was full of odd things like that,' said Anne. 'What other things are there like that, do you think? Let's ask her.'

They went back into the kitchen.

'Mrs Sanders, what other funny things are there in this house?' asked Julian.

'Well,' said the old lady, 'let me see.'

Go to **57**.

53

'Timmy! Timmy, come back!' shouted George.

But Timmy took no notice, and soon he was out of sight behind a small clump of bushes. George ran after him, but when she got to the bushes there was no sign of him!

'Timmy!' she called again. 'Timmy!'

The others came rushing up to her.

'Where has he gone?' asked Dick. 'I can't see him anywhere.'

'He's probably gone down a rabbit hole and got stuck,' said George. 'And if he's stuck, we'll probably have to dig him out, and then we'll never get to Kirrin Farm before lunch.'

'Well, I think we'd better split up and look for him,' said Julian. 'Why don't you and Dick go off that way, George? Anne and I can follow the path.'

If you think Anne and Julian will find Timmy, go to 60. If you think Dick and George will find him, go to 41.

54

If you have arrived from 35, score ⌒⌐.

Mrs Sanders took the lid off the tin, and there inside was a batch of the most delicious-looking shortbread. All the children ate at least two pieces with their cocoa, and Dick managed four! Timmy was not forgotten, either. Mrs Sanders found a big dog biscuit, and he sat on the rug in front of the range, gnawing happily.

'Ah, the wife's been very busy this week,' said Mr Sanders. 'She's been baking all sorts of things.'

'Oh, are you going to have company this Christmas?' asked George.

Go to **58**.

55

Timmy lay down again on the rug, watching the cat out of narrowed eyes.

'Doesn't Timmy like cats, George?' asked Anne.

'Not very much,' replied George. 'He's a very good, obedient dog in most ways, but he *loves* chasing cats!'

'Well,' said Julian, 'I think it's time that we all went home for lunch. Aunt Fanny did ask us not to be late. Thank you very much for the cocoa and shortbread, Mrs Sanders.'

'That's all right, my dear,' said the farmer's wife. 'Do come back and see us again another day, won't you?'

They all trooped out into the hall.

Go to **59**.

56

'What's behind the panel?' asked Julian.

The hole was about the width of his head, and when he stuck his head inside he could see only darkness. The wall itself was about twenty centimetres behind the panelling; it was made of stone.

'Get a torch, do get a torch,' said Anne, thrilled.

'There's one on the kitchen mantelpiece,' said Mrs Sanders. Anne shot off to get it.

Julian shone the torch into the hole behind the panel. The others pushed against him to try and peep inside.

'Don't,' said Julian impatiently. 'Wait your turn.'

'Maybe you'll find some treasure in there,' suggested Anne. 'I bet you will!'

*If you think Julian finds some treasure, go to **66**. If not, go to **52**.*

57

*If you have arrived from **61**, score* ⌔ ⌔.

The children all looked at Mrs Sanders eagerly.

'There's a cupboard upstairs with a false back,' she said. 'Don't look so excited! There's nothing in it at all! And there's a big stone over there by the fireplace that pulls up to show a hidey-hole. I suppose in the old days people wanted good hiding-places for things.'

The children ran to the stone she pointed out. It had an iron ring in it, and was easily pulled up. Below was a hollowed-out place, big enough to take a small box. It was empty now, but it looked exciting.

'Where's the cupboard?' asked Julian.

*Go to **62**.*

'Yes, we're having people to stay,' said Mr Sanders. 'Two artists from London are coming down.'

'I should think they'll be rather lonely down here in the depths of the country at Christmas-time,' said George. 'Do they know anyone?'

'Not a soul,' replied Mrs Sanders. 'But I've had one or two artists here before, and they seem to like going about all alone. I dare say these two will be happy enough.'

She chattered on to the children as she bustled about the big kitchen. Timmy, meanwhile, had finished his biscuit and was lying quietly on the rug. Suddenly he saw a cat slink into the kitchen, and he sat up with a growl, ready to chase the intruder.

'Timmy, lie down!' shouted George as Timmy got to his feet.

If you think Timmy lies down, go to **55**. *If you think he chases the cat, go to* **51**.

59

The children were just saying goodbye when Timmy suddenly noticed the tabby cat crouching in a corner, its eyes blazing and tail swishing. Timmy pricked up his ears and sprang towards it, but the cat spat angrily at him and reached out a paw to scratch his nose. Timmy jumped back and collided with the wall, hitting one of the polished panels. And then a most extraordinary thing happened!

The panel disappeared.

Go to **63**.

60

Anne and Julian set off along the narrow path, calling Timmy's name as loudly as they could. Their voices carried clearly in the frosty air. There was no sign of Timmy, and after they'd walked quite a long way Julian stopped and looked at Anne.

'I don't think he can be anywhere near here,' he said. 'He couldn't have got that far ahead of us. I think we'd better go back and join the others.'

Just then they heard Dick calling: 'Anne! Julian! Come here quickly!'

Go to **47**.

61

Gradually the dirt was rubbed away. The coin had worn very thin and flat, so it was difficult to see what had been engraved on it. They all studied it very closely until at last Anne's sharp eyes discovered the date.

'Eighteen thirty-five,' she said. 'Well, that's not very old. It's only a Victorian coin.'

'No, it's not,' said Julian. 'Queen Victoria didn't come to the throne until 1838. It's William IV. I don't suppose it will be valuable, but it's an interesting find.'

They all felt rather disappointed, but soon brightened up when George asked Mrs Sanders if there were any more odd panels or doors in the house.

'Well,' said the old lady. 'Let me see.'

Go to **57**.

62

'Up the stairs, turn to the right, and go through the second door you see,' said Mrs Sanders. 'The cupboard is at the far end. Open the door and feel about at the bottom until you come across a dent in the wood. Press it hard, and the false back slides to the side.'

The four children and Timmy ran upstairs as fast as they could. This really was a very exciting morning!

They found the cupboard and opened the door. All four children went down on hands and knees to press around the bottom of the cupboard to find the desired place.

'I've got it!' yelled Julian.

'I've found it!' shouted Anne at the same time.

If you think Julian has found the right place, go to **67**. *If you think Anne has found it, go to* **71**.

If you have arrived from **59**, *score* ⌒.

'What's happened?' cried Julian.

'Timmy fell against the wall,' said George, 'and the panel moved. And look – there's a dark sort of hole behind it.'

'It's a secret panel!' shouted Dick in excitement, peering into the hole. 'Golly! Did you know there was one there, Mrs Sanders?'

'Oh yes,' replied Mrs Sanders. 'This house is full of funny things like that. I'm very careful when I polish that panel, because if I rub too hard in the top corner it always slides back.'

Go to **56**.

Go to **56**.

64

The panel slid back, and Dick stepped out. After that all the children took turns at going into the space behind the back of the cupboard and being shut up. Anne didn't like it very much.

'Well,' said George eventually, 'we'll be late for lunch if we don't hurry. I think we'd better go down and find Mrs Sanders.'

Go to **68**.

Dick took out his head and put in his arm, stretching along the wall as far as his hand could reach.
He was just about to take it back when his fingers
found a hole in the wall.

'Funny!' thought Dick. 'Why should there be a
hole in the stone wall just there?'

He stuck in his finger and thumb and worked
them about. He felt a little ridge inside the wall,
rather like a bird's perch, and was able to get hold
of it. He wriggled his fingers about the perch, but
nothing happened. Then he got a good hold and
pulled.

The stone came right out! Dick was so surprised
that he let go the heavy stone and it fell to the
ground behind the panelling with a crash!

Go to **76**.

Julian shone the torch slowly all over the wall
behind the panel, but there didn't seem to be
anything there. It was difficult to see very much,
because the torch lit up only a small area of the
wall at a time.

Julian withdrew his head from the hole and put
his arm through and felt around the wall. It was
very frustrating, because he couldn't shine the
torch into the hole and put his arm in at the same
time!

'Oh, I'm sure there must be treasure in there,' said Anne again.

Just then, Julian's fingers touched something that felt like a small ledge. He ran his fingers along it carefully, and suddenly he felt something . . .

Go to **70**.

67

Julian pressed hard at the dent in the wood at the bottom of the cupboard, but nothing happened. He tried again, but the back of the cupboard remained firmly in place.

'Do you think you've got the right place?' asked George.

'I'm sure I have,' replied Julian. 'There's a big dent here. Perhaps the false back is stiff from lack of use.'

'But Mrs Sanders made it sound as if it were quite easy to get the back to move,' objected George. 'Well, try once again, and if it still won't move we'll try the place that Anne's found.'

So Julian pressed the dent again, but nothing happened.

'Come on,' George said to Anne. 'Press the dent you found!'

Go to **71**.

If you have arrived from **78**, *score* ⌒.

They went down to the warm kitchen again.

'It's the most exciting cupboard, Mrs Sanders,' said Julian. 'Can we come and explore it again?'

'No, I'm afraid you can't, Julian,' said Mrs Sanders. 'That room where the cupboard is – that's one of the rooms the two artists are going to have.'

'Oh,' said Julian, disappointed. 'Will you tell them about the sliding back, Mrs Sanders?'

'I don't expect so,' said the old lady. 'It's only you children who get excited about a thing like that.'

Go to **74**.

If you have arrived from **81**, *score* ⌒.

'Oh look, it's an old book,' said Dick.

'What's in it?' asked Anne.

They turned the pages carefully. They were so dry and brittle that some of them fell into dust.

'I think it's a book of recipes,' said Anne, as her sharp eyes read a few words in the old, brown faded handwriting. 'Let's take it to Mrs Sanders.'

The children carried the book to the farmer's wife, who took it and looked at it, not at all excited.

'Yes,' she said, 'it's a book of recipes, that's all it is.'

The children all felt disappointed. They had hoped that it would be something much more exciting than a book of old recipes!

'Do you think there's anything else in that hidey-hole?' said Anne. 'Come on, Julian! Let's go and see.' She dragged him back into the hall.

Julian put his arm into the hole in the wall.

Is there anything else in the hole? If you think there is, go to **79**. *If not, go to* **85**.

70

It was a round object, smooth and flat. Julian picked it up and pulled his arm out of the hole. He opened his hand, and there on his palm lay an old, tarnished coin!

'Golly!' shouted Dick. 'You *have* found some treasure!'

'Well, it's only one coin,' said Julian. 'I don't think there are any more in there. It was lying on a small ledge.'

'Yes, but some old coins are terribly valuable,' said George. 'This one has obviously been there a long time, too.'

'We'd better try to clean it up a bit,' said Julian. 'Have you got any silver polish, Mrs Sanders?'

'Yes, my dear,' said Mrs Sanders. 'Come in the kitchen and I'll find it.'

They all followed Mrs Sanders out to the kitchen, and watched breathlessly as Julian started to clean the old coin.

Go to **61**.

71

If you have arrived from **67**, *score* ⌒△.

Anne pressed hard. There was a creaking noise, and the children saw the false back of the cupboard sliding sideways. A big space showed behind, large enough to take a fairly thin man.

'A jolly good hiding-place,' said Julian. 'Anyone could hide in there and no one would ever know!'

'I'll get in and you shut me up,' said Dick. 'It'll be exciting.'

He got into the space. Julian slid the back across, and Dick could no longer be seen.

'Bit of a tight fit!' he called. 'And awfully dark! Let me out again!'

Anne gave a sudden shiver. She hated the idea of being shut up in the dark, and thought Dick was very brave. Then she had an awful thought. 'Suppose the panel sticks and we can't get Dick out?' she said.

'Oh, it'll be all right,' said Julian. 'It opened quite easily the first time we tried it.'

And he pressed the dent in the wood.

*If you think the panel opens easily, go to **64**. If you think it refuses to open, go to **75**.*

72

They all stared at each other in dismay. The hole was much too small for any of them to climb through – even Anne, who was small and slim.

Julian, who had the longest arms, tried standing on the chair and squeezing his shoulders through the hole, but it wouldn't work. It really began to seem as if they wouldn't be able to get the mysterious object out of the hole!

Then suddenly George gave a gasp and dashed off to the kitchen, calling to Mrs Sanders.

*Go to **82**.*

If you have arrived from **77**, *score* ◯.

As they walked into the kitchen Aunt Fanny was just carrying a dish through to the dining-room.

'Hello,' she said. 'You're just in time for lunch. Go and wash your hands quickly, and then come and sit down.'

After lunch the four children went upstairs to the boys' bedroom and spread out the bit of linen on the table there. It looked very strange and exciting.

Go to **84**.

'How funny,' said Anne. 'I'm sure I shall be thrilled to see a sliding panel or a trapdoor even when I'm a hundred!'

'Same here,' said Dick. 'Could I just go and look into the sliding panel in the hall once more, Mrs Sanders? I'll take the torch.'

Dick didn't know why he suddenly wanted to have another look. It was just an idea he had. He went into the hall and pressed on the panel at the top, and it slid back. He put the torch inside and had another look. There was nothing to be seen.

Go to **65**.

Nothing happened. Julian pressed again. Still nothing happened.

'I say!' called Dick. 'Hurry up and let me out of here, Julian! It's very dark and stuffy, and there's no room to move at all.'

'We can't get the panel open!' shouted Anne before Julian could stop her. He thought Dick might get in a panic if he knew they couldn't get him out.

'Shut up, Anne!' he muttered furiously. 'We don't want to frighten Dick!'

But Dick was a sensible boy, and he kept his head.

'I'm going to try pushing the panel from this side,' he shouted. 'Maybe that will move it.'

Go to **78**.

76

The noise brought the others out into the hall.

'Whatever are you doing, Dick?' asked Julian. 'Have you broken something?'

'No,' said Dick. 'I put my hand in here and found a hole in one of the stones the wall is made of – and I got hold of a sort of ridge with my finger and thumb and pulled. The stone came right out, and I got such a surprise I let go. It fell, and that's what you heard!'

'Golly!' said Julian, trying to push Dick away from the open panel. 'Let me see.'

'No, Julian,' said Dick. 'This is *my* discovery. Wait until I see if I can feel anything in the hole. It's difficult to get at!'

Dick put his arm in as far as he could, and curved his hand around to get into the space behind where the stone had been. His fingers felt about, and he closed them around something that felt oblong and smooth.

'I can feel something,' he said excitedly. 'It's sort of oblong-shaped.' Cautiously and carefully he began to bring the object out of the hole.

'Perhaps it's a book,' suggested George.

'Or a secret sort of box,' said Anne.

If you think it's a book, go to **69**. *If you think it's a box, go to* **81**.

77

There was no one in the kitchen, though all sorts of delicious smells were coming from the oven, so they ran through into the hall and up the stairs. But just as they got to the top, Uncle Quentin came out of the bathroom.

'Ah, there you all are,' he said. 'I think lunch is ready, so you'd better go down to the kitchen and see if your aunt needs any help.'

The children felt rather disappointed at not being able to study the map straight away, but they were all hungry, especially Dick! They turned and trooped back downstairs.

Go to **73**.

78

Dick put his hands flat on the panel in front of him and pushed sideways as strongly as he could. But as the panel was only a few centimetres in front of him he couldn't exert much pressure on it, and it was no good.

'No luck,' he called to Julian. 'Sorry!'

'I think I'd better go and get Mr Sanders to help us,' said Julian. 'He'll probably be able to get the panel open. Hold on, Dick. I shan't be long.'

Just before turning to go downstairs he gave the dent an exasperated kick, and the panel slid quietly back! Dick stepped out, grinning with relief.

'How did you make it work?' he asked Julian.

'I gave it a good kick,' said Julian, laughing. 'Come on, let's go downstairs and find Mrs Sanders.'

Go to **68**.

79

Julian's hand groped about, feeling for anything else that might be there. There *was* something else, something soft and flat that felt like leather.

Eagerly his fingers closed over it and he drew it out carefully.

'I've got something!' he said, his eyes gleaming with excitement. 'Look – what is it?'

It was a tobacco pouch, dark brown, made of soft leather and very worn. Carefully Julian undid the flap and unrolled the leather.

A few bits of black tobacco were still in the pouch – but there was something else, too!

Go to **88**.

80

George stuck her head in the hole while Julian held the torch for her. Julian was quite right – there was nothing to see except the wall.

'Well, it isn't very exciting,' she said, and started to pull her head out. As she did so she knocked Julian's hand, which was holding the torch, and the beam of the torch suddenly lit up the floor. The stone that Dick had pulled out was lying there, but George thought she could see something else, a dark, oblong shape, lying beside it.

'There's something on the floor next to the stone!' she shouted.

'What is it?' asked Anne excitedly.

'I can't see,' said George. 'We'll have to pick it up.'

'But how are we going to do that?' asked Dick. 'The hole is only big enough to get our heads in!'

Go to **72**.

'Oh look, it *is* a box!' said George. 'I wonder what's in it?'

The box was smooth and shallow, rather like a cigar-box. There was a small catch on the side, but it was rusty and snapped off as soon as they tried to open the box. It had a damp, musty smell, as if it had been behind the stone for a very long time.

The lid was slightly twisted with the damp, but George soon prised it up with her penknife. They all felt very excited about what they might find inside.

Go to **69**.

When she came back she was holding in her hand the long brass tongs that Mrs Sanders used for putting coal on the fire in her sitting-room.

'Look!' she said in excitement. 'I bet these can pick up whatever is in there.'

'What a clever idea,' said Julian. 'Well done, George!'

It took a long time to pick up the object, because it kept slipping out of the end of the tongs and falling on the floor again, but eventually Julian managed it, and he drew the tongs carefully out of the hole.

'What is it?' asked Anne. 'It looks a bit like Father's tobacco pouch.'

It *was* a tobacco pouch, very dark brown and made of soft, worn leather. Carefully Julian undid the flap and unrolled the leather.

A few bits of black tobacco were still in the pouch – and something else, too!

Go to **88**.

83

Mrs Sanders looked carefully at the piece of linen with its strange marks. She shook her head. 'No – this doesn't make any sense to me. But my husband would like this old tobacco pouch – his is just about worn out.'

'Mrs Sanders, do you want this piece of linen too?' asked Julian anxiously. He was longing to take it home to study it. He felt certain there was some kind of exciting secret hidden there.

'No, you take it, Julian, if you want to,' said Mrs Sanders with a laugh. 'I'll keep the recipes for myself, and John shall have the pouch. And now you'd best be going, because it must be your lunchtime!'

'Gracious! We'll be late! Come on, everybody!' said Julian. 'Goodbye, Mrs Sanders – and thank you!'

Go to **90**.

There were words here and there on the piece of linen, scrawled in rough printing. There was the sign of a compass, with E clearly marked for East. There were eight rough squares, and in one of them, right in the middle, was a cross. It was all very mysterious.

'You know, I believe these words are Latin,' said Julian, trying to make them out. 'But I can't read them properly. And I expect if I *could* read them I wouldn't know what they meant. I wish we knew someone who could read Latin like this.'

'Could your father, George?' asked Anne.

'I expect so,' said George.

But nobody wanted to ask George's father. He might take the curious old rag away. He might forget all about it; he might even burn it. Scientists were such odd people.

'What about Mr Roland?' said Dick. 'He's a tutor. He knows Latin.'

'We won't ask him until we know a bit more about him,' said Julian cautiously. 'He *seems* quite jolly and nice – but you never know. Oh blow, I wish we could make this out, I really do.'

'There are two words at the top,' said Dick, and he tried to spell them out. 'VIA OCCULTA. What do you think they mean?'

Go to **89**.

Julian's hand groped about, feeling for anything else that might be there. But he couldn't find anything. It was quite a small hole, and if anything had been there he would have found it.

The children all felt disappointed. Such an exciting secret hiding-place really should have had something more thrilling than a book of old recipes in it!

'I'd like to have a look in there,' said George. 'You two boys have seen inside, but I haven't yet.'

'There's nothing much to see,' said Julian. 'But have a look if you like.'

Go to **80**.

Go to **80**.

86

If you have arrived from **104**, *score* ◯.

The door opened and Mr Roland looked in.

'Hello, hello!' he said. 'I wondered where you all were. What about a walk over the cliffs?'

'We'll come,' said Julian, rolling up the old rag.

'What have you got there? Anything interesting?' asked Mr Roland.

'It's a . . .' began Anne, and at once all the others began to talk, afraid that Anne was going to give the secret away. She went red as she guessed why all the others had interrupted her so quickly.

Fortunately Mr Roland said no more about the

piece of linen he had seen Julian rolling up. He was looking at Timmy.

'I suppose he must come,' he said.

George looked at him in indignation.

'Of course he must come!' she said. 'We never go anywhere without Timmy.'

Go to **93**.

87

Thinking things over, Julian decided to tell Mr Roland. After all, he needn't say anything about the old bit of marked linen. So he told their tutor about the exciting things they had seen at the old farmhouse, but said nothing about the bit of linen. Mr Roland listened with the greatest interest.

'This is all remarkable,' he said. 'Very remarkable indeed. You say the old couple live there alone?'

'Well, they're having two people to stay over Christmas,' said Dick. 'Artists, I think.'

Go to **103**.

88

If you have arrived from **82**, *score* ⌒⌒ ⌒⌒ ⌒⌒.

Tightly rolled up in the last bit of pouch was a piece of linen. Julian unrolled it and put it flat on the hall table.

The children stared at it. There were marks and signs on the linen, done in black ink that had hardly faded. But the four of them couldn't make head or tail of the marks.

'It's not a map,' said Julian. 'It seems a sort of code or something. I wonder what it means. It must be some sort of secret.'

They ran to show it to Mrs Sanders.

'Look, what's this about, Mrs Sanders?' said George. 'Do you know?'

Go to **83**.

89

'Well, the only thing I can think of that they can mean is Secret Way or something like that,' said Julian.

'Yes, but they could mean something magic,' argued Dick. 'People talk about the occult when they mean ghosts and magic and things like that.'

'Perhaps it's a magic spell,' suggested Anne, her eyes shining.

'Well, I think it's Secret Way,' said Julian firmly. 'Magic spells don't work, everyone knows that!'

'I'm sure it means Magic Spell,' said Dick. 'I know! We'll get the dictionary from Uncle Quentin's study and see if that will help.'

'I'll go and get it,' said George, and ran out of the room. A minute later she was back with the big dictionary under her arm.

'Now,' said Julian, 'Dick says "Via Occulta"

means Magic Spell, and I think it's Secret Way. Let's see who's right.'

If you think Dick is right, go to **100**. *If you think Julian is right, go to* **96**.

90

The five of them dashed off quickly. They really were late and had to run most of the way, which meant that it was difficult to talk. But they were so excited about their morning they panted remarks to each other as they went.

'I wonder what this old rag says!' puffed Julian. 'I mean to find out. I'm sure it's something mysterious.'

'Shall we tell anyone?' asked Dick.

'No, let's keep it a secret,' said George.

'Well, we can have a good old puzzle of it after lunch,' said Julian as they ran up the garden path at Kirrin Cottage.

'Oh no,' said Dick. 'I can't wait until after lunch! Let's have a quick look at it now!'

If you think they should look at it straight away, go to **77**. *If you think they should wait until after lunch, go to* **73**.

91

Thinking things over, Julian decided it would be better not to tell Mr Roland. He wasn't quite sure whether he liked the tutor or not. Mr Roland

66

seemed very pleasant and jolly, but Julian thought it strange that Timmy would have nothing to do with him.

They walked on for a little way. Anne was walking beside Mr Roland, chattering to him about what she had been doing at school last term and what she hoped she might be given for Christmas. But then, to his dismay, Julian heard her start talking about their visit to Kirrin Farmhouse that morning.

Go to **95**.

92

If you have arrived from **101**, *score* ⌢.

As Mr Roland stretched out his legs, to his enormous surprise his feet struck something soft and warm – and then something nipped him sharply on the ankle! He drew in his feet with a cry of pain.

The children stared at him. He bent down and looked under the table.

'It's that dog,' he said in disgust. 'The brute snapped at my ankles. He has made a hole in my trousers. Take him out, Georgina.'

Go to **98**.

93

Mr Roland went downstairs, and the children got ready to go out. George was scowling. The very idea of leaving Timmy behind made her cross.

They all set out, Timmy too. Mr Roland needn't have worried about the dog, for Timmy wouldn't go near him. It was really very strange. Even when Mr Roland offered him a biscuit, he just put his tail down and went to George. Mr Roland gave up.

'He's a strange-looking dog, isn't he?' he said. 'A terrible mongrel!'

George went purple in the face with rage.

'He's *not* strange-looking!' she spluttered. 'He's the best dog in the world!'

Go to **99**.

94

'We'll go by bus into town and you can shop to your hearts' content,' said Aunt Fanny. 'Then we'll have tea in a tea-shop and catch the six o'clock bus home.'

The shops in the town looked gay and bright, and the children were very busy indeed buying all sorts of things. There were so many people to get presents for! Then they went to have tea.

They had a large and delicious tea. Aunt Fanny ordered all sorts of cakes for them. Dick was just about to eat his third éclair when Aunt Fanny looked at her watch. 'Goodness!' she exclaimed. 'It's ten to six! We'll have to hurry if we're going to catch the six o'clock bus!'

They dashed into the bus station just as their bus started to pull away.

Does the bus stop for them? If you think it does, go to **102**.
If you think it doesn't, go to **112**.

95

Soon Anne was telling Mr Roland about all the things they had found: the stone in the fireplace and the cupboard with the false back, and the sliding panel. Julian couldn't think of a way to make Anne stop!

'Oh well,' he said to himself, 'I suppose Mrs Sanders would tell anyone about all those things. They're not really secrets. I just hope Anne doesn't tell him about the bit of linen.'

Mr Roland listened to what Anne was saying with great interest.

'This is all remarkable,' he said. 'Very remarkable indeed. You say the old couple live there alone?'

'Well, they're having two people to stay over Christmas,' said Dick. 'Artists, I think.'

Go to **103**.

96

'We'll look up "via" first,' said Julian.

He searched through the dictionary until he came to the Vs.

'Vet . . . veto . . . via!' he said. 'The Latin word "via" means "way".'

'Now find "occulta",' said Dick.

Julian turned back to the Os and quickly found the right place.

'"Occult." It means hidden, or concealed!' he shouted triumphantly. 'There, I told you it meant Secret Way!'

Suddenly they heard footsteps coming along the passage.

Go to **86**.

97

Next morning the children felt a little gloomy. Lessons! How horrid in the holidays! Still, Mr Roland wasn't so bad. The children hadn't had him with them in the sitting-room the night before, because he had gone to talk to their uncle, so they were able to get out the mysterious bit of linen again and pore over it.

But it wasn't a bit of good. Nobody could make anything of it at all. It was most exasperating not to be able to find out.

'I really feel we'll have to ask someone soon,' Julian had said with a sigh. 'I can't bear this mystery much longer. I keep on and on thinking about it.'

He had dreamt of it, too, that night, and now it was morning – with lessons ahead. He wondered what lesson Mr Roland would take – Latin perhaps. Then he could ask him what the words VIA OCCULTA meant.

Mr Roland had seen all their school reports and noted the subjects they were weak in. One was Latin, and another was French. Only Anne was supposed not to need any coaching.

Go to **105**.

98

George said nothing. She sat as though she hadn't heard.

'She won't answer if you call her Georgina,' Julian reminded him.

'She'll answer me whatever I call her,' said Mr Roland in a low and angry voice. 'I won't have that dog in here. If you don't take him out this very minute, Georgina, I shall go to your father.'

George looked at him. She knew perfectly well that if she didn't take Timmy out, and Mr Roland went to her father, he would order Timmy to live in the garden kennel, and that would be dreadful. There was absolutely nothing to be done but obey.

Go to **107**.

99

Mr Roland took no notice of George. He just strode on ahead with the others, doing his best to be jolly. Soon they came in sight of the farm.

'That's Kirrin Farmhouse,' said Julian. 'We went there this morning. It's a very exciting place.'

Julian wondered whether to tell Mr Roland about all the things they had seen that morning. After all, Mrs Sanders was quite happy to tell anyone about the sliding panel and the stone in the kitchen. He hesitated. Should he say anything or not?

If you think Julian should tell Mr Roland, go to **87**. *If you think he should say nothing, go to* **91**.

100

Quickly Julian thumbed through the dictionary until he came to the Os. He ran his finger down the page.

'Here we are,' he said. 'Occult means hidden, or concealed!'

Dick was peering over Julian's shoulder at the dictionary.

'Look,' he said. 'On the next line it says that occult *also* means magic, so there!'

'Let's look up "via",' suggested George.

Go to **104**.

101

Julian, who was sitting next to Mr Roland, quickly asked him a question about the sum he was trying to do. As Mr Roland leaned over to look at Julian's book, he drew his legs back under his chair. The children all breathed a sigh of relief!

The lesson continued peacefully for a while, then Mr Roland put down his pen.

'Eleven o'clock!' he said. 'We'll have a short break now, and you can all have some cocoa and a biscuit.'

As he spoke he leaned back in his chair, stretching his arms and pushing his legs under the table!

Go to **92**.

102

Julian waved his arms and shouted at the driver: 'Hey! Wait for us!'

Luckily the driver saw him and stopped. The four children and Aunt Fanny climbed aboard and sat down thankfully. The bus rattled through the country lanes, and soon they were back at Kirrin Cottage.

Go to **110**.

103

If you have arrived from **95**, *score* ⌒⊣.

'Julian can paint awfully well,' went on Dick. 'He thought he might go over and talk to the artists one day.'

'Oh, I don't think he'd better go and worry the artists at the farmhouse. They might not like it,' replied the tutor.

This remark made Julian feel obstinate. He made up his mind at once that he *would* go and talk to the two artists when he got the chance.

'Now, home we go,' said Mr Roland. 'We shall just be in time for tea!'

Go to **97**.

104

Julian turned to the Vs.

'Vet . . . veto . . . via!' he said. 'The Latin word "via" means "way"!'

'Well, you can't have a magic way,' said George, 'so it *must* be Secret Way. Golly, how exciting!'

Just then they heard footsteps coming along the passage towards the bedroom.

Go to **86**.

105

'We shall start at half-past nine,' said Mr Roland. 'We are to work in the sitting-room. If you'd like to come along and join us, Anne, I'll give you some painting to do.'

So all the children were there, sitting around a table.

'Where's Timmy?' asked Julian in a low voice as they waited for their tutor to come in.

'Under the table,' said George defiantly. 'Don't any of you say anything about him.'

'Ssh!' said Dick. 'Here comes Mr Roland.'

Go to **109**.

106

They hadn't gone very far along the road when a lorry pulled up beside them. 'Did you miss the bus?' the driver asked them. It was Mr Sanders from Kirrin Farmhouse, driving home from market! They were all delighted to see him.

'You three climb in the back,' Mr Sanders said to Julian, George and Dick. 'Anne, you and your aunt climb in the cab with me.'

The two boys and George clambered into the back of the lorry. It smelt a bit from the pigs that Mr Sanders had taken to market, but nobody minded that!

Soon they were back at Kirrin Cottage.

Go to **110**.

107

Red in the face, a huge frown almost hiding her eyes, George got up and spoke to Timmy: 'Come on, Timmy! I'm not surprised you bit him. I would too, if I were a dog!'

'There is no need to be rude, Georgina,' said Mr Roland angrily.

George scowled, but took Timmy out and came back in a few minutes. The others were sorry for George and Timmy, but they didn't share her intense dislike of the new tutor. He often made them laugh, and he was patient with their mistakes.

After lessons that morning the children went out for half an hour in the frosty sunshine. George cheered up when she heard that they were all to go Christmas shopping that afternoon – without Mr Roland!

Go to **94**.

108

Luckily, Uncle Quentin wasn't paying any attention to Anne's chatter.

'If you're interested in my work, perhaps you would like to give me a hand,' suggested Uncle Quentin.

'Actually, we're supposed to be helping George and Dick with the Christmas tree,' said Julian.

'It won't take long,' said Uncle Quentin.

Go to **117**.

109

The tutor came in, his black beard bristling around his mouth and chin. He told the children to

sit down, and soon the little class was working away quietly. Anne was busy painting a bright picture of poppies and cornflowers.

Suddenly there was a huge sigh from under the table. It was Timmy, tired of lying so still. The children all began to make noises to hide the sounds that Timmy was making until he had settled down quietly again. Then Mr Roland stretched his legs out under the table. Julian and George looked at each other in dismay. Would he find Timmy under there?

If you think Mr Roland finds Timmy, go to **92**. *If you think he doesn't, go to* **101**.

If you have arrived from **106**, *score* ⌒ ⌒.

The next day there were lessons again from half-past nine to half-past twelve. George appeared without Timmy. She was angry at having to do this, but it was no good being defiant and refusing to come to lessons without Timmy. Now that he had snapped at Mr Roland, he had definitely put himself in the wrong, and the tutor had every right to refuse to let him come. But George looked very sulky indeed.

In the Latin lesson Julian took the chance to ask what he wanted to know.

'Please, Mr Roland,' he said, 'could you tell me what "via occulta" means?'

'"Via occulta"?' said Mr Roland, frowning. 'Yes. It means "secret path" or "secret road" . . . A hidden way – something like that. Why do you want to know?'

'Oh . . . I just wanted to know,' said Julian. 'Thank you.'

He winked at the others.

Go to **115**.

111

'Well, we want to know what the secret is, don't we?' asked Julian. 'We don't need to tell him where we got this, or anything about it, except that we want to know what the markings mean.'

'He'll want to know simply everything about it,' said George. 'He's terribly nosey. I saw him yesterday snooping around the study when no one was there. He didn't see me outside the window with Timmy. *Don't* show him the linen, Julian!'

'Well, *I* think you should,' said Dick.

Should they show Mr Roland the linen? If you think they should, go to **118**. *If not, go to* **127**.

112

Julian waved his arms and shouted at the driver: 'Hey! Wait for us!'

But it was no good. The driver didn't see him, and the bus pulled away into the chilly evening.

'Now what do we do, Aunt Fanny?' asked Anne in a worried voice.

'We'll just have to walk,' said Aunt Fanny. 'It's only a few miles. I'm afraid it'll take a long time, though. Your uncle will wonder what's happened to us. Perhaps he'll come and look for us in the car.'

Go to **116**.

113

Uncle Quentin looked at Anne in surprise. 'A secret way?' he said. 'What do you mean, a secret way?'

Anne went bright pink. 'Oh . . . er . . . yes . . . a secret way to . . . of . . . of making mince pies!' she stammered.

Julian pulled Anne out of the room before she had time to say anything else.

'Anne, the only way to stop you giving secrets away is to sew up your mouth!' he said. 'Come on, let's go and help the others with the decorations.'

They found George and Dick decorating the Christmas tree that Mr Roland had brought in earlier from the garden.

'I do think Mr Roland has been decent, digging up the Christmas tree and everything,' said Dick.

'Oh you're always on his side,' grumbled George. 'I'm going to go for a walk with Timmy. *He* knows what Mr Roland is really like.'

She stalked off in a huff. Dick shrugged his shoulders and said: 'What about asking Mr Roland if he can read that old linen rag for us?'

Go to **124**.

114

'Well, if you won't show the linen to Mr Roland, Julian, I jolly well will!' said Dick. Reaching over, he picked up the linen off the table.

'Dick!' shouted George. 'Put it back!'

'No!' Dick retorted crossly. 'I think you're being beastly about all this, George! You know how much we all want to know what the words mean!'

George made a grab at the piece of cloth in Dick's hand and nearly succeeded in pulling it away from him.

'Don't!' yelled Anne. 'You'll tear it!'

Just at that moment the door opened and Mr Roland walked in. Both George and Dick let go of the cloth and it fell to the floor.

'Well, well,' said the tutor, bending to pick it up. 'What's this, then?'

Go to **130**.

115

For the next day or two the four children didn't really have much time to think about the Secret Way, because Christmas was coming near and there was a good deal to do.

They went out with Mr Roland to find sprays of holly, and came home laden. That evening they decorated the house.

'Are you going to have your study decorated, too, Uncle Quentin?' asked Anne.

Go to **120**.

116

The children looked at each other. They knew that Uncle Quentin got very wrapped up in his work, and they suspected that he would never even notice that they weren't there. He would be too busy working on his secret formula or talking to Mr Roland. They'd have to walk all the way home, and they were all laden with Christmas shopping!

They set off along the road. Anne was tired after their busy afternoon, and she felt like crying at the idea of having to walk such a long way. Julian noticed her worried face.

'Cheer up, Anne!' he said. 'Here, let me carry some of your parcels for you.'

Anne handed Julian some of her shopping and he walked along beside her, talking to her to try to keep her spirits up.

Go to **106**.

117

There was a huge pile of files on Uncle Quentin's desk, with bits of paper sticking out of them. They all had funny names on them.

'What do all those names mean, Uncle Quentin?' asked Julian.

'They are all chemicals that I am using in my experiments,' his uncle replied. 'Perhaps you two would put them back in alphabetical order for me.'

Anne and Julian tidied the files, then put all the scientific instruments neatly in a box, and lined up all the test-tubes tidily in their racks.

Uncle Quentin was reading a large, dusty book, and only grunted when Julian told him that they had finished. They left the study and found George and Dick decorating the Christmas tree that Mr Roland had dug up earlier in the day.

'I do think Mr Roland has been decent, digging up the Christmas tree and everything,' said Dick.

'Oh you're always on his side,' grumbled George. 'I'm going to go for a walk with Timmy. *He* knows what Mr Roland is really like.'

She stalked off in a huff. Dick shrugged his shoulders and said: 'What about asking Mr Roland if he can read that old linen rag for us?'

Go to **124**.

118

Just at that moment the tutor came into the room.

'Mr Roland,' began Julian, ignoring George's furious glare, 'could you help us with something?' He handed over the piece of linen.

'Well, well,' said the tutor. 'What's this, then?'

Go to **130**.

119

'What is it, Timmy?' whispered George.

Timmy went on growling softly. George sat up and put her hand on his collar to stop him. She knew that if her father woke up he would be cross. Timmy stopped growling now that he had roused George. She sat and wondered what to do. Should she just ignore Timmy and go back to sleep? Or should she go to see if everything was all right downstairs?

If you think she should go back to sleep, go to **121**. *If you think she should get up, go to* **126**.

120

'No, my study is certainly not to be messed about,' said Uncle Quentin at once.

'Uncle, why do you have all those funny things in your study?' asked Anne.

Uncle Quentin laughed. 'I'm looking for a secret formula!' he said.

'You want to know a secret formula, and we want to know a Secret Way,' said Anne, quite forgetting that she wasn't supposed to talk about it.

Julian frowned at Anne, then glanced at his uncle. He was sure Uncle Quentin would ask Anne what she meant!

If you think Uncle Quentin asks Anne about the Secret Way, go to **113** *If he takes no notice of her, go to* **108**.

121

George was sure that Timmy wouldn't have started to growl without a reason, but she was very sleepy after the long, exciting, day. Staying in her warm bed seemed much nicer than walking through the cold, dark house! She lay down again and was asleep within half a minute.

But Timmy didn't go back to sleep. He sat up, ears pricked, head on one side, listening intently. Softly he began to growl again. Then he nudged George's arm through the bedclothes until she woke up again.

'What is it, Timmy?' she said. 'Do let me go back to sleep!'

Go to **128**.

122

'Well, Timmy must go outside and live in the kennel,' said George's father. 'I'm not having him in the house.'

'I won't let Timmy live outside,' said George furiously. 'It's such cold weather.'

'It will depend entirely on your behaviour from now on whether Timmy is allowed in the house at all these holidays! I shall ask Mr Roland each day how you have behaved. If you have a bad report, then Timmy stays outside. Go back to bed, but first apologise to Mr Roland!'

'Oh please, Father, don't send Timmy outside. Please let me keep him in for tonight!' begged George.

Does George persuade Uncle Quentin to let Timmy stay inside? If you think she does, go to **129**. *If you think she doesn't, go to* **138**.

123

If you have arrived from **135**, *score* ◯∀.

'All the rooms downstairs have stone floors,' said Mrs Sanders. 'You hunt all you like, my dears. But don't go into the room upstairs with the cupboard that has a false back, will you, or the one next to it. Those are the rooms the two artists have.'

'Which side of the house faces east, Mrs Sanders?' asked Julian.

'The kitchen faces due north,' said Mrs Sanders. 'So east will be over there,' she pointed to the right.

The three children walked out of the kitchen in the direction she had shown them. There were four rooms there – a kind of scullery, a tiny room used as a den by Mr Sanders, a room that had once been used as a drawing-room, and a store-room.

'Which room should we explore first?' asked Anne.

'How about the scullery?' suggested Dick.

If you think they should explore the scullery first, go to **139**. *If not, go to* **144**.

124

If you have arrived from **117**, *score* ◯∀.

'I'd *love* to ask him,' said Anne. 'He's most awfully clever. I'm sure he could tell us what the Secret Way is.'

'All right,' said Julian. 'I'll show him the piece of linen. It's Christmas Eve, and this evening Aunt Fanny is going into the study with Uncle Quentin to wrap up presents for all of us, so Mr Roland will be with us in the sitting-room.'

That evening, before Mr Roland came in to sit with them, Julian took out the little roll of linen and stroked it out flat on the table. George looked at it in surprise.

'Mr Roland will be here in a minute,' she said. 'You'd better put it away quickly.'

'We're going to ask him what the Latin words mean,' said Julian.

'You're not!' cried George in dismay. 'Ask him to share our secret! However can you?'

Go to 111

125

Mr Roland sent Anne to borrow a magnifying glass from her uncle. As soon as she got back, the four of them looked through the glass and saw the words three times as clearly as before.

'Well,' said the tutor at last, 'as far as I can make out, the directions mean this: a room facing east; eight wooden panels, with an opening somewhere to be found in that marked one; a stone floor – yes, I think that's right, a stone floor; and a cupboard. It all sounds most extraordinary and very thrilling. Where *did* you get this?'

'We just found it,' said Julian after a pause. 'Oh

Mr Roland, thanks awfully. We could never have made it out by ourselves. I suppose the entrance to the Secret Way is in a room facing east.'

'It looks like it,' said Mr Roland, poring over the linen roll again. 'Where did you say you found this?'

'We didn't say,' said Dick. 'It's a secret, really, you see.'

'I think you might tell me,' said the tutor, looking at Dick with his brilliant blue eyes. 'I can be trusted with secrets. You've no idea how many strange secrets I know.'

'Well,' said Julian, 'I don't really see why you shouldn't know. We found it at Kirrin Farmhouse, in an old tobacco pouch. I suppose the Secret Way begins somewhere there! I wonder where, and wherever can it lead to? We must look for the entrance to the Secret Way after Christmas.'

'I'll come with you,' said Mr Roland. 'I may be able to help a little. That is – if you don't mind me having a share in this exciting secret.'

'Well, you've been such a help in telling us what the words mean,' said Julian, 'we'd like you to come if you want to.'

Go to **133**.

126

Perhaps I'd better go and see if everything is all right, thought George. She was quite fearless, and the idea of creeping through the still, dark house didn't disturb her at all. Besides, she had Timmy! Who could be afraid with Timmy beside them?

She slipped on her dressing-gown.

Perhaps a log has fallen out of one of the fire-places, and a rug is burning, she thought, sniffing as she went down the stairs. There had been fires in both the sitting-room and the dining-room, as well as in the kitchen range. Where should she look first?

If you think George should start in the dining-room, go to **131***. If you think she should start in the sitting-room, go to* **137***.*

127

Julian looked at them both. He badly wanted to know what the words on the linen roll meant, and he was sure that the tutor would be able to help them. On the other hand, he didn't want to upset George.

'All right, George,' he said, 'I won't show Mr Roland the linen if you're so against it.'

'Oh *Julian!*' wailed Anne. 'Now we'll never know what the words mean!'

Go to **114***.*

128

Then George sat up again and listened. She still couldn't hear anything, but Timmy obviously could. She would have to get up and see whether anything was wrong. She slipped on her dressing-gown.

Perhaps a log has fallen out of one of the fire-places, and a rug is burning, she thought, sniffing as she went down the stairs. There had been fires in both the sitting-room and the dining-room, as well as in the kitchen range. Where should she look first?

If you think George should start in the dining-room, go to **131**. *If you think she should start in the sitting-room, go to* **137**.

129

George's father looked at her in exasperation. He wanted to go back to bed, not deal with a defiant little girl and an angry tutor!

'Very well, George,' he said at last. 'Timmy may stay in for tonight, but he's going outside tomorrow. Whether he's allowed in again will entirely depend on you. Now, apologise to Mr Roland!'

'No!' said George.

Go to **136**.

130

If you have arrived from **114**, *score* ⌒⊲.

'It's an old bit of linen,' explained Julian. 'It's got some rather odd markings on it. The words seem to be in Latin and we can't make them out.'

George went out of the room and shut the door with a bang. Nobody took any notice of her.

'Where in the world did you get this? What an odd thing!' remarked Mr Roland as he laid the piece of cloth out flat on the table. 'Ah – I see why you wanted to know the meaning of those Latin words the other day, the ones that meant "hidden path". They are at the top of this linen roll.'

'We just want to know the meaning of the words,' said Julian.

'This is really very interesting,' said the tutor, puzzling over the linen. 'Apparently there are directions here for finding the opening or entrance to a secret path or road.'

'That's what we thought!' said Julian excitedly.

'These eight squares are meant to represent wooden boards or panels, I think,' said the tutor, pointing to the eight rough squares drawn on the linen.

The children hung on his words. Wooden panels! That must mean panels somewhere at Kirrin Farmhouse.

Go to **125**.

131

If you have arrived from **128**, *score* ◌⟋.

With her hand on Timmy's head to warn him to be quiet, George crept through the hall and into the dining-room. The embers of the fire glowed red in the hearth, but the guard was in front of the fire and everything was fine. There was a large bowl of fruit on the table, and George took a tangerine. In spite of all she had eaten during the day, she felt hungry! She peeled the tangerine and offered a piece to Timmy.

'There you are, Timmy,' she whispered. 'Come on, we'll look in some of the other rooms.'

But Timmy took no notice. He started to growl again, and George could feel the hair on the back of his neck standing up!

Go to **141**.

132

'No, not right now. I want to run down to the village first to get something. But I'll meet you at the farmhouse later,' replied the tutor.

So the three children set off, wishing that George were with them.

Old Mr and Mrs Sanders were pleased to see them.

'Well, have you come to find a few more secret things?' asked Mrs Sanders with a smile.

'May we try?' said Julian. 'We're looking for a room that's facing east, with a stone floor and panelling!'

Go to **123**.

The next day was Christmas Day. The children awoke early and tumbled out of bed to look at the presents that were stacked on chairs near by. They spent a glorious hour before a late Christmas breakfast opening all kinds and shapes of parcels. The bedrooms were in a fine mess when the children had finished!

It really was a jolly Christmas Day. There were no lessons, of course, and the children gave themselves up to the enjoyment of eating a great deal, sucking sweets, and playing with their Christmas presents.

They were all tired out when they went to bed.

'It's been lovely,' said George, jumping into bed. 'Here comes Mother to say goodnight. Basket, Timmy!'

Timmy leapt into his basket by the window. He was always there when George's mother came to say goodnight to the two girls. As soon as she had gone downstairs, however, he took a flying leap and landed on George's bed. There he fell asleep, his head curled around her feet.

Two hours later everyone else was in bed. The house was still and dark when suddenly George woke up with a jump. Timmy was growling!

Go to **119**.

Mr Roland tried to get up, but Timmy wouldn't let him. George's father called to him sternly: 'Timmy! Come here!'

Timmy glanced at George to see if his mistress agreed with her father's command. She said nothing, so Timmy took no notice of the order and merely made a snap at Mr Roland's ankles.

'That dog's mad!' said Mr Roland from the floor. 'He's already bitten me once before, and now he's trying to do it again!'

'Timmy! Will you come here!' shouted George's father. 'George, that dog is really disobedient. Call him off at once.'

'Come here, Timmy!' said George in a low voice. The dog at once came to her.

The tutor got up. He was very angry indeed.

'I heard some sort of noise and came down with my torch to see what it was,' he said. 'I thought it came from your study, and I wondered if some thief was about. I'd just got into the room when that dog appeared from nowhere and got me down on the ground!'

'What is this I hear about Timmy biting Mr Roland before?' asked George's father angrily.

'George had him under the table during lessons,' said Mr Roland. 'I didn't know that, and when I stretched out my legs he bit me! Both George and the dog have tried to annoy me ever since I came here.'

Go to **122**.

They set off down the front path. The sea sparkled in the winter sunshine, and in the distance they could see Kirrin Island, its ruined castle standing out very clearly.

They hadn't gone very far along the path behind Kirrin Cottage which led across to the farmhouse when Mr Roland suddenly stopped.

'My goodness!' he exclaimed. 'I'd completely forgotten that I have to go down to the village for something. You three go on ahead and I'll see you at the farmhouse later.'

The tutor turned back towards the village, and the children walked on. Mr and Mrs Sanders were very pleased to see them.

'Well, have you come to find a few more secret things?' asked Mrs Sanders with a smile.

'May we try?' said Julian. 'We're looking for a room that's facing east, with a stone floor and panelling!'

Go to **123**.

136

George glared at her father, angry and upset. Even the thought of poor Timmy being put outside in the bitter weather could not persuade her to apologise to the tutor.

'Georgina! Apologise to Mr Roland or else!' ordered her father.

'I won't!' said George, and, choked by feelings of fury and dismay, she tore out of the room and up the stairs.

Go to **142**.

137

If you have arrived from **128**, *score* ⌢.

George walked through the hall to the sitting-room. The fire was quite all right there – just a red glow. The big Christmas tree stood in one corner, its glittering tinsel catching the light from the red embers on the hearth. It filled the room with a lovely smell of pine.

'Well, there's nobody in here, Timmy,' whispered George. 'Shall we go and look in the study next or the dining-room?'

If you think they should look in the study next, go to **150**. *If you think they should first look in the dining-room, go to* **131**.

138

'No!' said her father. 'Now say you are sorry to Mr Roland, then go back to bed!'

'I won't!' said George, and, choked by feelings of anger and dismay, she tore out of the room and up the stairs.

The two men stared after her.

'I'm sorry about all this,' said George's father. 'Now – what am I to do about that tiresome dog tonight?'

'Leave him for now,' said Mr Roland. 'I can hear noises upstairs – the others are awake by now! Don't let's make any more disturbance tonight.'

'Perhaps you're right,' said George's father, and the two men went back to bed.

Go to **142**.

139

The scullery was cold and bare. It had an old stone sink with a sloping wooden draining-board and a cold tap. There was a small window, very high up in the wall opposite the door. As Mrs Sanders had said, the floor was stone.

The three children looked around eagerly.

Go to **145**.

140

'Yes, I should like to come with you,' said the tutor. 'I feel I could do with a walk after all I ate yesterday!'

The three children put on their anoraks, scarves and gloves. It was a very cold, frosty morning, and they were all looking forward to a walk in the crisp air. The idea of looking for the Secret Way was very exciting, too! They ran downstairs just as Mr Roland came out of the study, where he had been talking to Uncle Quentin.

'Are you ready?' he asked.

Go to **135**.

141

George stood frozen to the spot. A scratching noise was coming from the window, as if someone was tapping quietly on the pane.

'It's only the wind blowing a branch against the window,' she said to herself. She walked over to the window and pulled the thick velvet curtain back. And there on the window ledge was an unusual sight!

Go to **146**.

142

If you have arrived from **136**, *score* ⌒↘.

The others were awake when George got back upstairs, and she told them what had happened. Anne began to cry. She hated hearing that Timmy was to be punished.

'Don't be a baby,' said George. '*I'm* not crying, and it's *my* dog!'

But when everyone had settled down again in

bed, and they were all peacefully asleep, George's pillow was very wet indeed.

Go to **148**.

143

It was Mr Roland! He was rolling on the floor trying to get away from Timmy, who was holding him firmly by his dressing-gown.

'Oh it's you, George! Call your beastly dog off!' said Mr Roland. 'Do you want to rouse the entire household?'

'Why are you creeping about with a torch?' demanded George.

'I heard a noise and came down to see what it was,' said Mr Roland.

'Why didn't you put on the light?' asked George.

'I couldn't find it,' said the tutor. 'It's on the wrong side of the door, you see.'

This was true. The switch was an awkward one to find if you didn't know it.

Then George's father appeared carrying a large poker. He stood still in astonishment when he saw Mr Roland on the ground and Timmy standing over him.

'What's all this?' he exclaimed.

Go to **134**.

144

'We don't need to look in the scullery,' said Julian.

'Why not?' asked Anne.

'Because the walls are made of stone, silly, and we want panelling,' said Julian. 'Use your brains, Anne! Now – let's start with the den.'

'Do you think we should go in there?' said Anne. 'After all, that's Mr Sanders' special room and I expect he's got private papers in there. Perhaps we should leave it alone. What do you think?'

If you think they should go into the den, go to **149**, *If you think they shouldn't, go to* **154**.

There was very little to see. There were two or three buckets on the floor under the sink, and some old saucepans, but otherwise the room was empty.

Suddenly Julian began to laugh.

'Well!' he exclaimed, chuckling. 'We are all silly. There's no point in us looking in here. We're looking for a room with panelled walls, and all the walls in here are stone!'

'Of course they are!' said Dick, laughing too. 'Now, shall we go into the den next?'

'Do you think we should go in there?' asked Anne. 'After all, that's Mr Sanders' special room and I expect he's got private papers in there. Perhaps we should leave it alone. What do you think?'

If you think they should go into the den, go to **149**. *If you think they shouldn't, go to* **154**.

146

An owl sat there, gazing at her with round, un-blinking eyes! The noise she had heard had been his beak tapping against the window pane. Feeling relieved, though she told herself that she hadn't really been frightened, she let the curtain go and crept out of the room, Timmy padding beside her.

'Now, Timmy, let's go and look in the kitchen,' whispered George.

But the kitchen was quiet and peaceful. Small crunching noises came from the range, the old clock ticked loudly, and everything was all right.

Go to **150**.

147

'Oh no, my dears,' said Mr Sanders. 'There's nothing in there that I want to keep private. You go in and explore. I don't mind at all.'

The den was panelled in dark oak, and the only furniture was an old bureau and a battered leather armchair.

'There must be some reason for putting *eight* squares of panelling in the directions,' said Julian, looking at the roll of linen again. 'It would be a good idea to see if there's a place with eight squares only – you know, over a window or something.'

Go to **159**.

148

There were no lessons the next day. George looked rather pale, and was very quiet. Timmy was already out in the kennel yard, and all the children could hear him whining unhappily. Mr Roland took no notice of George at all. The other children tried to bring her into their plans, but she remained quiet and uninterested.

'George! We're going over to Kirrin Farmhouse today,' said Dick. 'We're going to try to find the entrance to the Secret Way. Are you coming?'

George brightened. 'Yes – of course!' she said. But when she found that Mr Roland might be going with them too, she changed her mind at once. She would rather go for a walk with Timmy.

'Are you going to come with us, Mr Roland?' asked Dick.

If you think Mr Roland says yes, go to **140**. *If you think he says no, go to* **132**.

149

If you have arrived from **145**, *score* ◯⊰.

'Mrs Sanders didn't say we couldn't go in there,' said Julian, 'so I'm sure it will be all right. Come on!'

Mr Sanders' den was panelled in dark oak. The only furniture was an old bureau and a battered leather armchair.

'There must be some reason for putting *eight* squares of panelling in the directions,' said Julian, looking at the roll of linen again. 'It would be a good idea to see if there's a place with eight squares only – you know, over a window or something.'

Go to **159**.

150

If you have arrived from **146**, *score* ⌒ ⌒.

A slight sound came from the other side of the house.

Timmy growled quite loudly. George stood still. Could it possibly be burglars?

Suddenly Timmy shook himself free from her fingers and leapt across the hall, down the passage, and into the study beyond! There was the sound of an exclamation, and a noise as if someone was falling over.

'It *is* a burglar!' said George, and she ran to the study.

She saw a torch shining on the floor, dropped by someone who was even now struggling with Timmy.

Go to **143**.

151

'Let's try the store-room,' said Julian. 'It's bound to be smaller than the drawing-room, and we can look around it quickly.'

The store-room was full of brushes, mops and other odds and ends that Mrs Sanders used to clean the house. Hanging from the ceiling was an old birdcage, and on a shelf to one side was a huge preserving pan that Mrs Sanders used in the autumn for making jam and chutney.

Go to **169**.

152

The children all stared at the panel. It definitely didn't seem to fit as well as the others.

'I thought we'd checked every panel in the room,' said Julian. 'Anne, you were on this side of the room. Surely you looked at this one?'

'Well,' said Anne, 'I thought I did. Perhaps I missed it. Oh I know! I was just getting to that panel when Mr Wilton and Mr Thomas came in.'

Julian went over to the panel and started to tap it. It did sound rather hollow. Then he pressed it hard. Was it his imagination or did it move slightly?

If you think it moved, go to **161**. *If you think it didn't, go to* **168**.

153

If you have arrived from **169**, *score* ⌣.

The panelling in the drawing-room was different from the panelling in the den. It didn't look so old, and it wasn't so dark either. The squares were rather a different size, too.

The children tried each panel, tapping and pressing as they went, expecting at any moment to see one slide back as the one in the hall had done. But they were disappointed.

They were still in the middle of trying when they heard voices in the hall.

Go to **162**.

If you have arrived from **145**, *score* ⌒⧸.

'Mrs Sanders didn't say we couldn't go in there,' said Julian.

'Perhaps she thought we'd realise that it was private and leave it alone,' argued Anne.

They were standing in the passage, trying to decide whether or not to look in the den, when Mr Sanders came past.

'I thought you three would be busy exploring!' he said.

'Well, we weren't sure if we should go into your den or not,' said Anne. 'We thought it might be private. Do you mind if we do?'

If you think Mr Sanders lets them explore the den, go to **147**. *If you think he asks them not to, go to* **163**.

There was nothing in the space behind it except the bare stone wall. There was only a tiny space between the other panels and the wall, and not even Anne could get her hand into the gap.

'It looks as if this is just a panel that has come unstuck,' said Mr Roland. 'Put it back, Julian, and we'll go and say goodbye to Mrs Sanders.'

Julian fitted the panel back into the gap and they all went to find Mrs Sanders.

Go to **171**.

'Oh, it couldn't have been the artists you saw,' said
Anne at once. 'Mr Roland didn't know them. I had
to introduce them.'

'Well, I'm sure I heard Mr Roland call one of
them Wilton,' said George, puzzled. 'He *must* have
known them.'

'It couldn't have been the artists,' said Anne
again. 'They really didn't know Mr Roland. Mr
Thomas asked if he was a friend of ours.'

'I'm sure I'm not mistaken,' said George. 'If Mr
Roland said he didn't know the two artists, he was
telling lies.'

'Sh!' said Julian. 'Here he is.'

The door opened and the tutor came in.

'Well, Julian,' he said, 'how did you like the two
artists? I was pleased to meet them. They seem
nice fellows.'

George looked at the tutor. She felt sure it was
the artists she had seen him with. But why should
he pretend he didn't know them?

Go to **160**.

157

The men half bowed to one another and nodded.
'Are you staying here?' asked Mr Roland. 'A very
nice old farmhouse, isn't it?'

'It isn't time to go yet, is it?' asked Julian,
hearing a clock strike.

'Yes, I'm afraid it is,' said Mr Roland. 'I'm later meeting you than I expected. We must go in about five minutes. I'll just give you a hand in trying to find this mysterious Secret Way!'

But no matter how any of them pressed and tapped around the panels in the drawing-room, they couldn't find anything exciting.

'Well, we really must go now,' said Mr Roland. 'Come and say goodbye to Mrs Sanders.'

Just as they all turned to leave the room, Dick noticed a panel over by the window. It appeared somehow different from the others, as if it might be loose.

'Look!' he said, pointing to it. 'Have we checked that one?'

If you think they've checked the panel, go to **166**. *If you think they haven't, go to* **152**.

158

'Mr Roland, may I go out to see that Timmy is all right?' asked George, speaking so quickly that her words fell over themselves. 'I can hear him coughing, and it's *so* cold outside.'

Mr Roland looked at her. 'I don't think you can have been listening to what I just said about your work, Georgina,' he said. 'I am not having that dog in here, distracting you from your lessons and trying to bite me! I don't care how cold it is – he is not coming inside!'

Go to **174**.

*If you have arrived from **147**, score ⌓. If you have arrived from **167**, score ⌓ ⌓.*

It was tremendously exciting to look around the den! But though it certainly had panelled walls, and though they knocked and tapped in all sorts of places, they didn't find anything unusual. There was no place of only eight panels, either, as shown in the directions on the linen cloth.

They decided to go on to the next room.

'Now, shall we all go into the store-room next,' said Dick, 'or should we try the old drawing-room?'

*If you think they should all go into the store-room, go to **151**. If you think they should try the drawing-room, go to **165**.*

Next morning there were lessons again – and no Timmy under the table! The children could hear him whining outside as they worked. This troubled George even more than it did the others. Timmy was such a companion, and so dear to her, that she couldn't bear to think of him cold and miserable in the kennel yard. She sat chewing the end of her pencil and trying to make up her mind whether to ask Mr Roland if she could go to see if Timmy was all right. There was another whine from outside. George took a deep breath.

If you think George asks Mr Roland if she can go out to

Timmy, go to **170**. *If you think she decides not to, go to* **176**.

161

Julian pressed again. This time the panel moved upwards a couple of centimetres. The others gathered around in excitement. Julian pushed the panel again and it slid up a bit more, then fell forwards out of the wall!

Go to **155**.

162

Somebody looked into the drawing-room. It was a man, tall and thin, wearing glasses on his long nose.

'Hello!' he said. 'Mrs Sanders told me you were treasure-hunting. How are you getting on?'

'Not very well,' said Julian politely. He looked at the man, and saw behind him another one, younger, with rather screwed-up eyes and a big mouth. 'I suppose you're the two artists?' he asked.

'We are!' said the first man, coming into the room. 'My name is Thomas, and my friend's name is Wilton.'

Then a voice hailed them from the doorway. The children turned, and saw their tutor. The two artists looked at him.

'Is this a friend of yours?' asked Mr Thomas.

110

'Yes, he's our tutor, and he's very nice!' said Anne.

'Perhaps you will introduce me, Anne,' said Mr Roland, smiling at her.

'This is Mr Roland,' Anne said to the two artists. Then she turned to Mr Roland. 'This is Mr Thomas,' she said, waving her hand towards him, 'and the other one is Mr Wilton.'

Go to **157**.

163

Mr Sanders looked at the three children. 'Well, my dears,' he said. 'If you don't mind, I think I'd rather you didn't. There's nothing much in there. Just my old desk that I use when I'm seeing to the farm bills.'

'But the room is panelled, isn't it?' asked Julian.

'Oh yes,' replied Mr Sanders. 'It's panelled with oak all around.'

The children looked at each other. They all wanted to see inside the den, but none of them wanted to upset Mr Sanders if he didn't want them in there.

Just then Mrs Sanders came out of the kitchen and saw them all standing in the passage.

'What's the matter?' she asked. 'I thought you three would be tapping all the walls or some such carry on!'

Go to **167**.

164

George was back when they got to Kirrin Cottage.

'Did you discover anything?' she asked eagerly. 'Tell me all about it!'

'There wasn't anything to discover,' said Dick gloomily. 'There are two panelled rooms downstairs, and we went all around them, tapping and punching – but there was nothing there at all.'

'We saw the two artists,' said Anne. 'One was tall and thin and had a long nose with glasses on. He was called Mr Thomas. The other one, Mr Wilton, was younger, with little piggy eyes and an enormous mouth.'

'I saw them when I was out this morning,' said George. 'They didn't see me, but I'm sure it must have been them. Mr Roland was with them, and they were all talking together.'

Go to **156**.

165

Julian opened the drawing-room door and he and Anne went inside.

'I'll just have a quick look into the store-room,' said Dick.

He opened the store-room door and peeped inside, but it had stone walls, like the scullery, so he knew it couldn't be the right room. He followed the others into the drawing-room.

Go to **153**.

'Oh yes,' said Julian, 'I looked at that panel very carefully. It's only loose because it's come unglued from the others. There's no space behind it.'

The others all looked disappointed. For a moment Dick and Anne had both thought that they might have found something after all!

'Come on,' said Mr Roland. 'We'll go and say goodbye to Mrs Sanders.'

Go to **171**.

'Mr Sanders has asked us not to go into his den,' explained Julian.

'Why ever did you say that?' said Mrs Sanders to her husband. 'There's no reason why the children shouldn't look in there!'

'Well . . . er . . . it's not very tidy,' said the farmer.

'Rubbish!' replied his wife, and opened the door of the den.

The room was panelled all the way around in dark oak. The only furniture was an old bureau and a battered leather armchair. Piled against the walls were stacks and stacks of old farming magazines.

'Oh John!' exclaimed Mrs Sanders. 'You told me you were going to take all those old magazines out and burn them! No wonder you didn't want the children looking in here. You were afraid they'd tell me about them!'

Mr Sanders looked sheepish, then he smiled. 'Well, you children can look in the den, and welcome,' he said. 'When you've finished I'll move these old papers.'

Go to **159**.

168

He pressed it again, but nothing happened.

'Come on, you two,' he said to Dick and Anne, 'come and help me push. I'm sure we can get this panel to move if we all try.'

114

But it was no good. No matter how hard they pushed, the panel wouldn't move. In the end they gave up.

'It's no good,' said Dick. 'I don't think there can be anything unusual about this panel. It's not as loose as it looks.'

'We must go now,' said the tutor, who had been watching their efforts with interest.

They all went through to the warm kitchen to say goodbye to Mrs Sanders.

Go to **171**.

169

'I don't think this is the right room,' said Dick. 'There's no panelling – only stone walls.'

'Let's try the drawing-room,' suggested Julian.

Go to **153**.

170

'Mr Roland,' began George.

'Get on with your work, Georgina,' said the tutor coldly. 'I must remind you that you are a long way behind in several subjects, and you have a lot of ground to make up. You certainly haven't done very much work so far!'

He went back to explaining a sum to Dick.

George was silent for a moment, then she heard Timmy give a cough.

Go to **158**.

171

If you have arrived from **168**, *score* ◁. *If you have arrived from* **155**, *score* ◁ ◁.

Mrs Sanders smiled at the children as they came into the kitchen. 'Well, dearies, did you find what you wanted?' she asked.

'No,' said Mr Roland, answering for them, 'we haven't been able to find the Secret Way after all!'

'The Secret Way?' said Mrs Sanders in surprise. 'What do you know about that, now? I thought it had all been forgotten. In fact, I haven't believed in that Secret Way for many a year!'

'Oh Mrs Sanders – do you know about it?' cried Julian. 'Where is it?'

'I don't know, dear. The secret of it has been lost for many a day,' said the old lady. 'I remember my old grandmother telling me something about it when I was smaller than any of you. But I wasn't interested in things like that when I was little. I was all for cows and hens and sheep.'

It was disappointing that Mrs Sanders knew so little. The children said goodbye and went off with their tutor, feeling that their morning had been wasted.

Go to **164**.

To the tutor's enormous surprise, George gave him
a smile when he came back into the room. This was
so unexpected that it puzzled him. He was even
more puzzled to find that George worked harder
than anyone else for the rest of the morning, and
she answered politely and cheerfully when he
spoke to her. He gave her a word of praise: 'Well
done, Georgina! I can see you've got brains.'

The others looked at her in admiration. George
must be finding it very difficult to behave as if Mr
Roland were a great friend when she really disliked
him so much.

Go to **184**.

173

Uncle Quentin frowned. 'I'm not going to allow
George to go on behaving like this,' he said. 'She
will have to work hard, and be polite and pleasant
to you for at least a week before I'll even consider
having that dog back in the house.'

'Well, I think that is very wise,' replied Mr
Roland. 'The dog is a bad influence on Georgina.
In fact, it might be best if he remained outside for
the rest of the holidays.'

The three children were horrified. How *could* Mr
Roland tell such lies about poor George? Perhaps
she'd been right about him all along!

Go to **179**.

George jumped to her feet, her blue eyes blazing with anger. 'I *will* go to see that Timmy is all right!' she shouted. 'I *will*, and you can't stop me!'

'Indeed I can stop you,' said Mr Roland furiously. 'I can go straight to your father and suggest that he gets rid of that dog of yours, since not only is the brute dangerous but he is making you disobedient as well!'

George sat down slowly. She knew that her father would listen to Mr Roland, and the thought of Timmy being sent away was quite dreadful.

When the ten-minutes break came, Mr Roland went out of the room for a little while.

Go to **180**.

175

'George has worked better than anyone else today!' said Mr Roland. 'I am really pleased with her.'

'Uncle Quentin,' said Julian, 'George has tried awfully hard, she really has. And you know she's terribly unhappy about Timmy being out in the cold. He's got a dreadful cough. *Please* let him come indoors.'

'Well,' said Uncle Quentin, looking at the three eager faces before him, 'well . . . I hardly know what to say. If George is going to be sensible . . . What do you think, Roland?'

'I think you should keep to what you said and let the dog stay outside,' said Mr Roland. 'George is spoilt, and she needs firm handling. There is no reason to give way because she has tried to be good for once!'

The three children looked at one another in amazement, but said nothing. How mean of the tutor to stop Uncle Quentin from having Timmy indoors again! They all felt very disappointed in him.

Go to **179**.

176

'Stop sitting there with your mouth open and get on with your work, Georgina,' said Mr Roland sharply.

George bent her head over her books, tears in her eyes. She jolly well wasn't going to ask Mr Roland a favour now! She knew he'd say no, that she must get on with her lessons and leave Timmy alone.

When the ten-minute break came, Mr Roland went out of the room for a little while.

Go to **180**.

177

George quickly put on a few clothes and crept downstairs. The whole house was quiet. She slipped out into the yard. Timmy was delighted to see her and licked her hands and face lovingly.

She was just undoing his chain when suddenly Timmy gave a low growl. George felt the hair on the back of his neck stand up.

'What is it, Timmy?' she whispered. Straining her ears, she thought she heard a noise from the other side of the house, near the kitchen. George hesitated, wondering whether to go and see if there was anyone there.

If you think George should go and investigate the noise, go to **193**. *If you think she should take Timmy straight in out of the cold, go to* **187**.

178

'No,' said George, 'I'm not coming to lessons, and that's that!'

'But George,' said Julian, 'listen to me. We know you're very upset about Timmy, and we know that you hate Mr Roland, but being disobedient won't help you to get Timmy allowed back in the house, will it? It will only make things worse.'

George looked at Julian for a moment, then sighed. 'All right,' she said, sitting down at the table. 'I can see that what you've said makes sense, so I'll stay. But I'm not going to be polite to Mr Roland!'

Go to **194**.

If you have arrived from **173**, *score* ⌒.

Uncle Quentin looked at the tutor.

'Perhaps you'd like to come along to my study,' he said. 'I've got a bit further with my formula. It's at a very interesting stage.'

The two men went out of the room. George came in a moment later, her face eager. But when she saw the gloomy looks of the other three, she stopped short.

'Isn't Timmy to come in?' she asked quickly. 'What's happened? Tell me!'

They told her. George's face grew dark and angry when she heard what the tutor had said.

'Oh what a beast he is!' she cried. 'How I hate him! I'll pay him out for this. I will, I will, I will!'

She rushed out of the room, and in a moment they heard the front door bang.

'I bet she's gone to Timmy,' said Julian. 'Poor old George. She'll be worse than ever now.'

Go to **183**.

If you have arrived from **174**, *score* ⌒ ⌒.

Dick spoke to George: 'Listen – you just hate Mr Roland, and I suppose you can't help it. But we can none of us bear Timmy being out there all alone – and it looks like snow today, which would be awful for him. Could you be awfully, awfully good today and forget your dislike, so that Mr Roland can say you were very good when your father asks him for your report. And then we'll all ask Mr Roland if he'll let Timmy come back into the house.'

George looked at Dick for a moment.

'All right,' she said. 'I do hate Mr Roland. But I love Timmy more than I hate the tutor – so for Timmy's sake I'll pretend to be good and sweet and hard-working. And then you can beg him to let Timmy come back.'

Go to **172**.

181

'Timmy!' hissed George as loudly as she dared. 'Timmy! Come back here!' George was terrified that Timmy's barking would wake the grown-ups.

'Timmy, come here!' she called again.

There was a movement near the fence, and a low, shadowy shape slid along the path. George chuckled to herself. It was a fox, a big dog fox with a thick, bushy tail. No wonder the contents of the dustbin were all over the yard. Foxes were great scavengers and liked nothing better than turning out a dustbin!

The fox slid under the fence and out of sight. Timmy walked back to where George was standing, a rather wistful look on his face. He would have loved to chase that fox!

Go to **187**.

182

'George, don't behave fiercely today, will you?' said Julian after breakfast. 'It won't do you or Timmy any good at all.'

'Do you suppose I'm going to behave properly when I know perfectly well that Mr Roland will never let me have Timmy indoors all these holidays?' said George.

'Oh George,' said Julian with a sigh. 'We like you, and we hate you to be unhappy. We can't have any fun either, if we know you are miserable – and Timmy too.'

'Don't worry about *me*,' said George in rather a choky voice. 'I'm going out to Timmy. I'm not coming to lessons today.'

'Oh please come to lessons! You'll only get into *more* trouble if you don't!' begged Anne.

If you think George refuses to go to lessons, go to **189**. *If you think she decides to join the others, go to* **178**.

183

That night George couldn't sleep. She lay and tossed in her bed, listening for Timmy. She heard him cough. She heard him whine. He was cold, she knew he was. Suddenly she could bear it no longer. She must, she simply must get up and go down to him.

I shall bring him into the house for a little while and rub his chest with some of that stuff Mother uses for herself when she's got a cold, thought George. Perhaps that will do him good.

Go to **177**.

184

'George, you go out of the room before your father comes in to ask Mr Roland about your behaviour tonight,' said Julian later. 'Then, when the tutor gives you a splendid report, we'll all ask if Timmy can come back. It will be easier if you're not there.'

'All right,' said George. She was longing for this difficult day to be over.

George disappeared from the room just before six o'clock, when she heard her father coming. He walked into the room and nodded to Mr Roland. 'Well? Have your pupils worked hard today?'

'Very well indeed,' said Mr Roland. 'Julian has really mastered something he didn't understand today, and Dick has done well in Latin.'

'What about George?' asked Uncle Quentin.

'I was coming to Georgina,' said Mr Roland.

Dick looked at Anne and smiled. At least this time Mr Roland would have something nice to say about George! Or would he?

Is Mr Roland going to tell the truth about George? If you think he is, go to **175**. *If you think he's going to lie, go to* **188**.

185

Lessons went on. Break came, and still George didn't appear. Julian slipped out and saw that the kennel was empty. So George had gone out with Timmy!

No sooner had the children settled down after break to do the rest of the morning's lessons than there was a big disturbance.

Suddenly they heard the sound of a man talking to Aunt Fanny in a very loud, excited voice.

Mr Roland got up and opened the door.

If you think the voice belongs to Uncle Quentin, go to **192**. *If you think it belongs to someone else, go to* **197**.

186

Mr Sanders watched anxiously.

'Shut the gate, Dick,' he said. 'That'll stop the others getting out. I'm going to go and help Julian and Anne catch that blasted sheep.'

Dick shut the gate, and Mr Sanders puffed up the lane and on to the main road, where Julian and Anne were trying to chase the sheep back down the lane.

'Go on, you old so-and-so!' Mr Sanders shouted,

waving his stick at the sheep. It stopped and looked at him for a moment, then ambled slowly back down the lane, followed by the two children and Mr Sanders. Dick had opened the gate again, and now he quickly shut it behind the runaway animal. Mr Sanders mopped his brow.

'Thank you all very much, children,' he said. 'You were a great help. You'd better go back to your lessons now, but come over to Kirrin Farm again soon, won't you?'

The children went back through the garden and into the house. As they went down the passage to the sitting-room, they heard voices.

Go to **192.**

187

If you have arrived from **181**, *score* $\bowtie$ $\bowtie$.

Then Timmy gave a hollow cough. It sounded so dreadful that George thought she must get him into the house as quickly as she could.

'Come along into the warm for a little while,' she whispered. 'I'll rub your chest with some oil I've got.'

Timmy pattered behind her into the house. There was still quite a nice fire in her father's study, so she and Timmy went in there. She didn't put on the light, because the firelight was fairly bright. Sitting down on the hearth-rug, she rubbed the dog's hairy chest with the oil, hoping it would do him good. Then Timmy stretched out on the rug, and George settled down with her head on his neck. It was warm and peaceful, and both of them quickly fell asleep.

Go to **191**.

188

'I'm sorry to have to tell you that Georgina has done very little work today, as usual,' said Mr Roland. 'And she has been rude and unco-operative.'

Anne gasped, and Julian and Dick stared at Mr Roland in amazement. They could hardly believe their ears! George had been so good, and had worked so hard, and now Mr Roland was lying to her father, saying she had done very little! What was Mr Roland up to? Julian opened his mouth to tell his uncle that the tutor was lying, but then he decided not to say anything. Uncle Quentin would believe the tutor, not him. Grown-ups always stuck together.

Go to **173**.

189

'No,' said George, 'I'm just not going to come. I won't work with Mr Roland until he says I can have Timmy indoors again.'

'But you know you can't do things like that. You'll be punished!' said Dick.

'I shall run away if things get too bad,' said George in a shaky voice. 'I shall run away with Timmy.'

She went out of the room and shut the door with a bang.

Go to **198**.

190

Julian and Anne spread out their arms and yelled at the sheep as it trotted towards them. Then they began to walk towards it, and it turned around and ambled off down the lane and through the gate. Dick quickly closed the gate, and Mr Sanders mopped his brow.

'Thank you all very much, children,' he said. 'You were a great help. You'd better go back to your lessons now, but come over to Kirrin Farm again soon, won't you?'

The children went back through the garden and into the house. As they went down the passage to the sitting-room, they heard voices.

Go to **192**.

191

George awoke to hear the clock striking six! The room was cold, and she shivered. Goodness! Six o'clock! Her mother would soon be awake, and she mustn't find George and Timmy in the study!

'Wake up, Timmy! I must put you back in your kennel,' whispered George.

The two of them slipped out of the study, and soon Timmy was back in his kennel on the chain. George gave him a pat and went back indoors.

She went up to bed, sleepy and cold. She forgot that she was partly dressed, and got into bed just as she was. She was asleep in a moment!

A couple of hours later Anne was amazed when George got out of bed with most of her clothes on.

'Look!' she said. 'You're half dressed!'

'Be quiet,' said George. 'I went down and let Timmy in last night. We sat in front of the study fire and I rubbed him with oil. Now don't you dare say a word to anybody! Promise!'

Anne promised and they went down to breakfast.

Go to **182**.

192

If you have arrived from **190**, *score* ◁ ◁ ◁ ◁. *If you have arrived from* **186**, *score* ◁ ◁ ◁ ◁ ◁.

Uncle Quentin was standing in the passage talking to Aunt Fanny. He seemed upset and worried.

He looked at the three children. 'Have any of you been into my study?' he asked.

'No, Uncle Quentin,' they all answered.

'Well, the test-tubes I set yesterday for an experiment have been broken – and, what is worse, three most important pages of my book have gone,' said Uncle Quentin. 'Are you *sure*, children, that none of you has been meddling with things in my study?'

Go to **204**.

193

The noise came again more loudly. Timmy got up and stood listening, his head cocked to one side. He was still growling softly.

'Come on, Timmy,' whispered George. 'I think we'd better go and have a look.'

Moving as quietly as she could, George went around the back of the house to the yard outside the kitchen. The moon was shining brightly, and she could see quite clearly. One of the big dustbins lay on its side, the contents scattered all around the yard! And then Timmy suddenly gave a loud bark and rushed past George.

Go to **181**.

194

Julian sat down beside George and spread out his books. He felt a bit cross with George, even though he understood how she felt. But why couldn't she see that being sulky and disobedient wouldn't help?

George sat and stared out of the window. It was a cold day. There had been a heavy frost the night before, and now the sky was blue and clear. Then suddenly she heard a noise from the yard where Timmy was chained up. 'Timmy's coughing again,' she said, jumping up. 'I must go and see how he is!'

'Mr Roland will be here in a minute,' said Dick. 'You'd better be quick!'

'I've changed my mind,' said George. 'I'm not going to stay and do lessons with someone who forces my dog to live outside in this cold weather. I'm going out to Timmy, and I'm not coming back!'

She went out of the room and shut the door with a bang.

Go to **198**.

195

'We don't know. She didn't come to lessons this morning,' replied Mr Roland.

'Didn't come to lessons! The naughty girl! Fanny! Come here! Did you know that George hasn't been to her lessons today?'

Aunt Fanny came into the room. She held a little bottle in her hand.

'Didn't come to lessons!' repeated Aunt Fanny. 'Then where is she?'

'I don't think you need to worry about her,' said Mr Roland smoothly. 'What is very much more important, sir, is the fact that your work appears to have been spoilt by someone. I only hope it is not George, who has been spiteful enough to pay you out for not allowing her to have her dog in the house.'

'Quentin, I am sure that George would not even *think* of such a thing,' said Aunt Fanny. 'But I found this in your study.'

And she held up the little bottle she carried.

Go to **199**.

196

Mr Roland and Aunt Fanny went out of the room.

'I don't know if Mr Roland thinks he's coming out with us,' said Julian in a low voice, 'but we've got to get out first and give him the slip. We've got to find George and warn her what's up.'

The three children threw on their outdoor clothes and crept out of the garden door quietly. They raced towards the cliffs, and looked to see if George was coming.

'There she is – and Timmy too!' cried Julian, pointing. 'George, George! Quick, we've got something to tell you!'

Go to **205**.

Mr Sanders was standing in the passage, talking to Aunt Fanny. He looked rather hot and excited.

'Hello, Mr Sanders,' said Mr Roland. 'Is something the matter?'

'Yes,' said Mr Sanders. 'Someone has left the gate into the field open, and my sheep are all over the lane. Goodness knows how I'll get them back into the field. My old sheepdog Sam has hurt his paw, and I've had to leave him at home. Is George here? Maybe she and Timmy could help me round up the sheep.'

'George isn't here at the moment,' said Julian quickly. 'She's . . . er . . . taken Timmy for a walk. But we'll help you round up the sheep, Mr Sanders, if Mr Roland doesn't mind!'

Go to **201**.

198

If you have arrived from **194**, *score* ⌒⊣.

Mr Roland came into the sitting-room, his books in his hand. He smiled at the three children.

'Well? All ready for me, I see. Where's George?'

Nobody answered. Nobody was going to give George away.

'Gone to feed that dog of hers, I suppose,' said Mr Roland.

They all settled down. The time went on and

George didn't come. Mr Roland glanced at the clock and made an impatient clicking noise with his tongue.

'Really, it's too bad of George to be so late! Anne, go and see if you can find her.'

Anne looked everywhere but she couldn't find George. She went back and told Mr Roland. He looked angry.

'I shall have to report this to her father,' he said.

Go to **185**.

199

'Uncle Quentin took the bottle and stared at it. 'Camphorated oil?' he said. 'Well, *I* didn't put it there.'

'Who did, then?' asked Aunt Fanny, puzzled. 'None of the children has a cold. It's most extraordinary!'

Anne went very red again as she looked at the oil.

Mr Roland stared hard at the little girl.

'Anne, you know something about that oil!' he said suddenly. 'Did you put it there?'

Anne said nothing.

'I think she's shielding George,' said Mr Roland. 'Is that it?'

Anne stared at the ground. Should she continue to say nothing or make up a story that would stop the grown-ups suspecting George?

134

If you think Anne should make up a story to shield George, go to **203**. *If not, go to* **209**.

200

'No,' said George after a moment. 'If I'm going to get into a row, I'll get into it now! *I'm* not afraid!'

She marched over the cliff path, Timmy running around her as usual. The others followed. It wasn't nice to think that George was going to get into such trouble.

Mr Roland saw them from the window and opened the door. He glanced at George.

'Your father wants to see you in the study,' said the tutor.

George went to the study door and opened it. There was no one there.

'Father isn't here,' she said.

'Go in and wait,' said Mr Roland. 'And you others, go up and wash for lunch.'

George sat down to wait for her father.

Go to **207**.

201

'No, no,' said the tutor, 'I don't mind. We can finish our lessons later. You three go and help Mr Sanders.'

The children quickly got their anoraks and went

out into the garden. It was good to get out into the cold, clear air.

The lane was full of sheep wandering up and down aimlessly.

'Now,' said Mr Sanders, 'you go down that end, Julian, and stop them going any further down the lane. Anne, you go with him. Dick, you come and stand by the gate, and close it quickly as soon as the last one has gone through.'

'If he counts them as they go through he may fall asleep,' said Julian, grinning.

Go to **206**.

George walked slowly along the cliff, looking out at the cold sea. The sky was very grey and heavy now, and she wondered if it were going to snow.

She walked on for a little while then looked at her watch. It was very nearly time for lunch. She whistled to Timmy, who was sniffing at a rabbit hole, and started to walk home. No matter how much she told the others that she wasn't scared, she hated the thought of a row.

Go to **217**.

Anne took a deep breath. 'Well,' she began, 'I . . . er . . . was coughing a lot last night, and I thought I might be getting a cold, so I got the oil out of the bathroom cabinet to rub on my chest.'

'But why did you take it down to the study?' asked Aunt Fanny. 'Why didn't you do it in your bedroom?'

'Well, I didn't want to disturb George,' replied Anne. 'I thought that if I put the light on, it would disturb her.'

Mr Roland looked at Anne hard.

'And where did you leave the bottle when you had finished rubbing the oil on your chest?'

'Oh . . . er . . . I . . . on the table!' stammered Anne.

'Now we know you are not telling the truth,' said Aunt Fanny. 'I found the bottle by the study fender. Why are you trying to protect George?'

Go to **209**.

204

'Quite sure,' answered the children.

Anne went very red – she suddenly remembered what George had told her. George said she had taken Timmy into Uncle Quentin's study last night and rubbed his chest with oil! But George couldn't possibly have broken the test-tubes and taken pages from her father's book!

Mr Roland noticed that Anne had gone red.

'Do you know anything about this, Anne?' he asked.

'No, Mr Roland,' said Anne, blushing even redder.

'Where's George?' suddenly asked Uncle Quentin.

Go to **195**.

205

'What's the matter?' asked George as the three children tore up to her. 'Has something happened?'

'Yes, George. Someone has taken three most important pages out of your father's book!' panted

Julian. 'And broken the test-tubes he was making an experiment with. Mr Roland thinks you might have something to do with it!'

'The beast!' said George, her blue eyes deepening with anger. 'As if I'd do a thing like that! Why should he think it's me, anyway?'

'Well, George, you left that bottle of oil by the study fender,' said Anne. 'I haven't told anyone at all what you told me happened last night, but somehow Mr Roland guessed you had something to do with the bottle of oil. But you didn't take any pages from the book Uncle Quentin is writing, and you didn't break anything in the study, did you?'

'Of course not, silly,' said George indignantly. 'I suppose I shall get into trouble now for taking Timmy into the study.'

'Hadn't you better stay out a bit longer, until everyone has calmed down a bit?' said Anne.

George hesitated. She knew there would be a row, but should she go back and face it now or do as Anne suggested and wait until things had calmed down?

If you think George decides to go back with the others, go to **200**. *If you think she waits until things have calmed down, go to* **212**.

206

Mr Sanders shouted and whistled at the sheep, and slowly they began to move through the gate. Julian and Anne waved their arms and shouted at any of the flock that tried to get past them, and soon the sheep were jostling each other to get back in to the field.

But just as the last two or three were approaching the gate, one of them decided to be difficult. Turning around, it headed off up the lane towards where Julian and Anne were standing.

'Quick, stop her!' yelled Mr Sanders. 'Don't let her go any further, or she'll get out on the main road!'

If you think Julian and Anne stop the sheep in time, go to **190**. *If not, go to* **210**.

207

If you have arrived from **217**, *score* ⌒⌒.

Her father came into the room, frowning and angry. He looked sternly at George. 'Were you in here last night, George?' he asked.

'Yes, I was,' George answered at once.

'What were you doing in here?' asked her father. 'You know you children are forbidden to come into my study.'

George explained about bringing Timmy into the study to rub his chest with oil because he had such a dreadful cough.

'Well, something very serious had happened,' said her father. 'Some of my test-tubes have been broken – and, worse than that, three pages of my book have gone. Did you have anything to do with it?'

'No, I did not,' said George, looking her father straight in the eyes.

'Very well,' said her father. 'And now tell me, why were you not at lessons this morning?'

'I'm not going to do lessons any more with Mr Roland,' said George. 'I simply hate him!'

Her father did not know what to do with George. He thought he had better have a word with his wife. He got up and went to the door.

'Stay here. I shall be back in a moment. I want to speak to your mother about you.'

Go to **221**.

208

'I have been talking to your mother,' said George's father. 'She agrees with me that you have been very disobedient, rude and defiant. We can't let behaviour like that pass, George. You will have to be punished. You will go to bed for the rest of the day, and you will not see Timmy for three days. I will get Julian to feed him and take him for a walk. If you persist in being defiant, Timmy will have to go away altogether.'

'Oh!' cried George. 'Timmy will be so miserable if I don't see him for three whole days.'

'There's nothing more to be said,' answered her father. 'Go straight upstairs to bed and think over all I have said to you.'

Go to **213**.

If you have arrived from **203**, *score* ⌒.

Anne burst into tears. Julian put his arm around his sister and spoke to the three grown-ups.

'*Don't* bother Anne. Can't you see she's upset?'

'We'll let George speak for herself when she comes in,' said Mr Roland. 'I'm sure she knows how that bottle got there. 'And if she put it there herself she must have been in the study – and she's the only person who *has* been there.'

'When George comes in, send her to me in my study,' said Uncle Quentin irritably, then he stamped out, cross and frowning.

Mr Roland shut the books with a snap.

'We can't do any more lessons this morning,' he said. 'Put on your things and go out for a walk until dinnertime.'

Go to **196**.

Julian and Anne spread out their arms and yelled at the sheep as it trotted towards them, but it was no good! The sheep ambled on up the lane past the children. Julian tried to grab hold of it as it went past, but he couldn't get a grip on it and he was left holding a handful of wool!

'Come on, Anne!' he shouted. 'We must try to catch it before it gets to the main road!'

The two of them started to run after the sheep, but, hearing the running feet behind it, the sheep began to charge up the lane at full speed!

Go to **186**.

211

George was very angry that anyone could think that she had broken the test-tubes, and she thought it was very unfair of her mother to be cross with her for being in the study, when Mr Roland had told her to go in there in the first place.

Really, she was having a horrible time these holidays! What with having to do lessons with a tutor she hated, not being allowed to have Timmy in the house, and now being accused of breaking the test-tubes, she rather wished she was back at school!

Go to **218**.

212

George hesitated for a moment. 'All right,' she said. 'I think I'll wait out here for a while with Timmy. You three had better go back to the house.'

Julian hated the idea of leaving poor George alone, knowing that she'd be in a great deal of trouble when she came back to the house, but he thought it was a good idea for her to wait until Uncle Quentin was less angry.

'Well,' he said, 'Don't be too long. You don't want to be late for lunch, as well as everything else!'

Go to **202**.

213

George went upstairs and undressed. She got into bed and thought miserably of not seeing Timmy for three days. She couldn't bear it! Nobody knew how much she loved Timmy!

No one came up to see her. George felt sure the other children had been forbidden to come near her. She felt lonely and left out. She thought of her father's lost pages. Could Mr Roland have taken them? After all, he was very interested in her father's work and seemed to understand it. The thief must have been someone who knew which were the important pages. Surely Timmy would have barked if a thief had come in from outside. He had such sharp ears.

I think it must have been someone *in*side the house, thought George. None of us children, that's certain – and not Mother! So that leaves only Mr Roland. And I did find him in the study that other night when Timmy woke me by growling.

Go to **223**.

'No, George, *don't*,' said Julian. 'Honestly and truly, it's awful to search somebody's room like that. And anyway, I dare say he's got the pages with him. He may even be going to give them to somebody.'

'I never thought of that,' admitted George, and she looked at Julian with wide eyes. 'Isn't that sickening? Of course he may be doing that. He knows those two artists at Kirrin Farmhouse, for instance. They may be in the plot, too.'

'Oh George, don't be silly,' said Julian. 'You're making a mountain out of a molehill, talking of plots and goodness knows what! Anyone would think we were in the middle of a big adventure.'

'Well, I think we are,' said George.

Julian stared at his cousin thoughtfully. Could there possibly be anything in what she said?

'Julian, will you do something for me?' asked George.

Go to **231**.

The floor was covered with a large thick carpet. George got up and went over to the wall. She began to pull up the edge of the carpet.

Just then she heard the sound of footsteps

coming down the passage towards the study, and the door started to open. George still had the edge of the carpet pulled back. Should she try to replace it or should she stay as she was and try to think of an excuse?

If you think she tries to replace the carpet, go to **224**. *If you think she leaves it as it is, go to* **229**.

216

But before George could think what to do, her mother came out of the bedroom.

'George!' said Aunt Fanny. 'What are you doing? You're supposed to be in bed.'

'I . . . er . . . wanted to go to the bathroom, Mother,' said George.

'Then why have you got your clothes on?' asked her mother. 'Surely you haven't been lying in bed in your clothes?'

'I was cold,' replied George. 'It's a very cold day – and there's no fire in my room, so I kept my clothes on.'

'Well, go back to bed,' said her mother. 'Undress, and if you are cold get an extra blanket from the cupboard. Really, between your bad behaviour and your father getting so cross about his broken test-tubes, I've got a terrible headache! Now go back to your room!'

Go to **222**.

As George walked into the house Mr Roland appeared.

'Georgina, did you go into the study last night?' asked the tutor, watching George as she took off her anorak.

'I'll answer my father's questions, not yours,' said George.

'What you want is a good spanking, and if I were your father I'd give it to you!' said Mr Roland.

'You're not my father,' answered George. She went to the study door and opened it. There was no one there.

'Father isn't here,' she said.

'He'll be there in a minute,' said Mr Roland. 'Go in and wait.'

George sat down to wait for her father.

Go to **207**.

Go to **207**.

218

If you have arrived from **211**, *score* ○◁.

George glared furiously at the closed door, then turned back to the carpet. As she pulled up the edge of it she saw that the floor underneath was made of large, flat stones. The study had a stone floor too, then!

She put the carpet back in place, then sat down again and gazed at the wooden panels, trying to remember which one in the roll of linen was marked with a cross. But of course it couldn't be a room in Kirrin Cottage – it must be in Kirrin Farmhouse where the Secret Way began.

But just suppose it *was* Kirrin Cottage! Certainly the directions had been found in Kirrin Farmhouse – but that wasn't to say that the Secret Way had to begin there, even though Mrs Sanders seemed to think it did.

George was feeling excited. I must tap around those eight panels and try to find the one that's marked on the linen roll, she thought. It may slide back or something, and I shall suddenly see the entrance opening!

She got up to try her luck – but at that moment the door opened again and her father came in, looking very grave.

Go to **208**.

219

'Ah, this will do!' George said to herself. She shot into the bathroom and closed the door, hearing what sounded like her mother's footsteps going along the landing. Carefully opening the door a crack, she looked out. Her mother was standing by the big cupboard on the landing, getting some aspirin out of her box of medicines. George shut the door again and waited until she heard her mother's steps going back along the passage, and the bedroom door closing. Then she slipped out of the bathroom and down the stairs.

Go to **233**.

220

George got out of bed. 'You stay here,' she said to Julian. 'Then if I get caught, no one can blame you.' And she slipped out of the room.

The door of Mr Roland's room creaked rather a lot as she opened it, and George was afraid that her mother would hear it, but nothing happened. She slid into the room and closed the door behind her.

The tutor's room was very tidy, with books piled on the table and his slippers placed neatly beside the bed. In the corner stood a briefcase.

Go to **228**.

221

The door closed. George sat still on her chair and gazed up at the mantelpiece, where a clock ticked away the time. She felt very miserable. She counted the wooden panels as she looked at the panelled overmantel. There were eight. Now, where had she heard of eight panels before? Of course – the Secret Way. There were eight panels marked on the roll of linen. What a pity there hadn't been eight panels in a wooden overmantel at Kirrin Farmhouse!

George glanced out of the window and wondered if it faced east. She looked to see where the sun was. It wasn't shining into the room, but it did in the early morning – so it must face east. Fancy – here was a room facing east with eight wooden panels. She wondered if it had a stone floor.

Go to **215**.

222

George turned and walked slowly back to her room. She felt that nobody cared about her any more, or about Timmy. Supposing Timmy was lying shivering in the snow with no one to rub him dry. He must be wondering why George didn't come to him. At the thought of Timmy losing the trust he had in her, George felt more miserable than ever. She got back into bed and buried her face in her pillow.

Go to **230**.

223

She sat up in bed suddenly. I believe Mr Roland had Timmy put out of the house because he wanted to go around the study again and was afraid Timmy would bark! she thought. He was so very insistent that Timmy should go out of doors – even when everyone else begged for me to have him indoors. I believe . . . I really do believe that Mr Roland is the thief!'

George lay back in bed and gazed out of the window, thinking how much she wished that the others could come to see her so that she could talk things over with them!

'Golly,' she said to herself suddenly, 'I think it's snowing! Poor Timmy, out there in the cold. I wonder if his kennel is clear of the drifting snow? I'll bet no one's thought about that. I wonder if I dare risk going down to see if he's all right?'

If you think George goes down to see that Timmy's all right, go to **236**. *If you think she stays in bed, go to* **230**.

224

George decided to try and replace the carpet, but as she pulled it back into place her elbow caught a pile of books on the desk and knocked them all on to the floor!

The door opened and Aunt Fanny came in.

'What do you think you're doing in here, George?' asked her mother crossly. Then, without waiting for George to answer, she went on: 'You know you children are forbidden to enter your father's study. And you've knocked over that pile of books, too. Pick them all up and then go upstairs and wash your hands for lunch. Really, I'm beginning to think that you might have knocked

over those test-tubes after all, you're so
clumsy!'

And with that she went out of the room.

Go to **211**.

225

'Oh George, I don't think you can be right,' said
Julian. 'It sounds so far-fetched and unbelievable.'

'Lots of unbelievable things happen,' said
George. 'Lots. And this is one of them.'

'Well, if Mr Roland did steal the pages, they
must be somewhere in the house,' said Julian. 'He
hasn't been out all day. They must be somewhere
in his bedroom.'

'Of course!' said George, looking thrilled. 'I
wish he'd go out! Then I'd search his room.'

'George! You can't do things like that,' said
Julian. 'Oh – what's that noise?'

There was the bang of a door. Julian peeped out
of the window.

'It's Mr Roland, going for a walk,' he said.

'Oooh – I could search his room now if you'll
keep watch at the window and tell me if he comes
back,' said George, throwing back the bedclothes.

'George! You can't do that,' said Julian
again.

'Oh, can't I?' said George.

If you think George searches Mr Roland's room, go to **220**.
If you think Julian persuades her not to, go to **214**.

'Really?' said Julian in delight. It had been a great disappointment to him that all their searching had come to nothing. 'All right – I'll try to creep up again later.'

He slipped downstairs, popped his head into the sitting-room and whispered to the others that he was going out after the tutor.

Then he found the white macintosh and went through to the kitchen. He had hoped to slip out without anyone seeing him, but Aunt Fanny was in the kitchen.

'I'm just going to see if Timmy's all right,' said Julian.

Go to **234**.

Go to **234**.

227

George crept to the door and opened it slowly. There was no one around. She stuck her head out and listened hard. She could hear the others talking in the sitting-room.

'Mr Roland is going for a walk, and Aunt Fanny is lying down,' she heard Dick say. 'I think Uncle Quentin is in his study, as usual, so perhaps the three of us could play cards for a while.'

Good! All the grown-ups were busy. George crept along the landing, her shoes in her hand. But just as she got to the top of the stairs she heard the door of her parents' bedroom opening! She looked around wildly for somewhere to hide.

If you think George manages to hide, go to **219**. *If you think she gets caught, go to* **216**.

228

George looked around the room. There were very few places to hide anything. There was a large wardrobe and a chest of drawers, but apart from that the only furniture was the bed and a small table. George decided to start with the chest of drawers.

She pulled open the top drawer and looked quickly under the stacks of socks and shirts it contained, but there was nothing there. Then she looked in the other two drawers, but all she found was more clothes. There was nothing much in the wardrobe either. That left only the briefcase. She picked it up and laid it on the bed.

'I bet it's locked,' George said to herself.

But it wasn't! She lifted the lid in excitement. Would there be anything inside?

If you think there is something in the briefcase, go to **232**. *If you think it's empty, go to* **238**.

229

The door opened and Aunt Fanny came in. 'What are you doing here, George?' she asked. 'And why have you got the carpet rolled back like that? Really, you have no business to be in your father's study at all!'

'I . . . I dropped my pencil,' said George, 'and I had to roll back the edge of the carpet to look for it.'

'Well, hurry up and find it, then,' said her mother crossly.

Giving George no time to explain that she was in the study because Mr Roland had told her to go in there to wait for her father, Aunt Fanny went on: 'I can't see why you're in here anyway. If you're in the habit of coming in here when you know you shouldn't, I can almost believe that it was you who broke the test-tubes!'

And with that she left the room.

Go to **218**.

230

If you have arrived from **222**, *score* ᑲ ᑲ ᑲ ᑲ.

Suddenly George heard a voice outside. It was Julian, talking to Timmy.

'Good old Timmy!' George heard him say. 'Are you all right? Let me sweep some of this snow away and swing your kennel around a bit so that no flakes fly inside. There – that's better. No, we're not going for a walk, old thing – not now.'

George felt very relieved. At least now she knew that Timmy was all right!

Go to **240**.

*If you have arrived from **238**, score* ⌒⌒. *If you have arrived from **239**, score* ⌒⌒⌒⌒.

'Of course,' said Julian at once.

'Go out and follow Mr Roland,' said George. 'Don't let him see you. There's a white macintosh in the hall cupboard. Put it on and you won't be easily seen against the snow. Follow him and see if he meets anyone and gives them anything that looks like the pages of my father's book – you know, those big pages he writes on.'

'All right,' said Julian. 'But I'm sure I shan't be able to follow Mr Roland anyway – he's been gone ten minutes now!'

'Yes, you will, silly – he'll have left his footmarks in the snow. And, oh, Julian – I quite forgot to tell you something else exciting,' said George. 'Oh dear, there isn't time now. I'll tell you when you come back, if you can come up again then. It's about the Secret Way.'

*Go to **266**.*

*Go to **266**.*

232

And there was! Inside the briefcase were three or four sheets of paper covered in odd numbers and symbols. George recognised Mr Roland's writing because she had seen it during lessons. She couldn't understand all the symbols, but they seemed to be for a chemical formula. There were one or two words written on the papers that she remembered hearing her father use when he told people about his work.

'Goodness,' said George to herself, her blue eyes blazing with excitement, 'I was right! Mr Roland must have copied these from my father's book! But these aren't the pages that were stolen from the study because they're not in Father's writing.'

She put the pages back in the briefcase and tiptoed back down the corridor to her own room.

Go to **235**.

233

George crept through the hall and into the deserted kitchen. Then she opened the back door and looked out. The snow was falling very heavily, and the whole garden was covered in a white blanket. Quickly she pulled on her shoes, then she walked around the corner of the house to where she could see the kennel. There was no need to worry about making a noise, because the snow muffled the sound of her footsteps.

She dared not go too close to the kennel. She was afraid that if Timmy saw her he would be so pleased that he would bark, and that might attract someone's attention. But from where she stood she could see that the kennel had been turned away from the snow. At least now she knew that Timmy was dry!

As quickly as she could, she crept back into the house and into her room.

Go to **240**.

234

'It's snowing fast and thickly,' said Aunt Fanny. 'If it goes on like this we shall be completely snowed up! The milkman and the baker won't be able to get to us. Fortunately I can bake my own bread, but we may run short of milk.'

Julian had an idea. 'Shall I go over to the farm and get some extra milk, Aunt Fanny?' he asked. 'It won't take very long.'

'Oh that would be a help,' said his aunt. 'But do be careful, won't you? Don't get lost.'

Julian set off down the path to the gate. He could follow the deep prints of Mr Roland's boots very easily in the clean snow. But when he got to the top of the lane he found another set of footprints that seemed the same size as the tutor's. One set of footprints went straight ahead, but the other went off to the left. Which should he follow?

If you think he should go straight on, go to **242**. *If you think he should turn left, go to* **246**.

235

'Julian! Guess what!' said George breathlessly. 'I found a briefcase in Mr Roland's room, and in it

158

were papers with a chemical formula on them. They aren't the papers that Father's lost because the writing is Mr Roland's, but he must have copied the formula from Father's book!'

'Oh George,' said Julian. 'You're letting your imagination run away with you. You know that Mr Roland is interested in scientific things – he's always going to talk to your father about his work. Those papers you found could be about any formula. There's no reason why they should be copied from your father's work!'

Go to **239**.

236

George lay in bed trying to make up her mind what to do. If she went down and got caught, she would be in worse trouble than she was already. But if she didn't go and check that Timmy's kennel wasn't filling with snow he might catch cold and be very ill. It was the thought of Timmy being ill that made up George's mind. She jumped out of bed and pulled on her clothes.

Go to **227**.

237

If you have arrived from **249**, *score* ◌.

Suddenly Julian heard the sound of voices and stopped. A big gorse bush lay to the right, and the voices came from there. He went nearer to the bush. He heard his tutor's voice talking in low tones. He couldn't hear a word that was said.

Whoever can he be talking to? he wondered. He crept up closer to the bush. There was a hollow space inside. Julian thought he could creep right into it and peer out of the other side.

Once inside the bush, he parted the prickly branches slowly and cautiously. To his amazement he saw Mr Roland talking to the two artists from Kirrin Farmhouse – Mr Thomas and Mr Wilton!

Go to **253**.

238

Much to George's disappointment the briefcase was empty. She closed the lid and put the case back by the wall. She really had thought that she would find the missing pages of her father's secret formula in Mr Roland's room, but there was nothing there.

She hurried out of the room and back to her own bedroom, where Julian was waiting for her.

'No luck,' she said. 'But I'm still sure that Mr Roland's involved in all this!'

George got back into bed and sat thinking for a minute. Then she looked up at Julian. 'I say, Julian, will you do something for me?' she asked.

Go to **231**.

George stared at her cousin. What he had said certainly made sense, but somehow she *knew* that the pages in the briefcase had been copied from her father's book.

George got slowly back into bed and sat thinking for a moment. Then she looked up at Julian.

'Julian, will you do something for me?' she asked.

Go to **231**.

If you have arrived from **233**, *score* ◁ ◁ ◁.

After a while the bedroom door opened and in crept Julian. He shut the door, and saw George sitting up in bed looking at him with delight.

'Sh!' said Julian. 'I'm not supposed to be here!'

'Oh Julian!' said George. 'How good of you to come. I was so lonely. Here – sit on the bed.'

George began to pour out to him all that she had been thinking of.

'I believe Mr Roland is the thief,' she finished. 'I really do!'

Go to **225**.

'By the way,' said the tutor in a very jolly voice. 'Guess who I just met? Those two artists from Kirrin Farmhouse. They had been out for a walk and got quite lost, poor fellows, so I put them on the right path back to the farmhouse.'

'Really?' said Julian. Obviously the tutor was afraid that Julian had seen him talking to the artists and was trying to explain what he had been doing!

They came to the gate of the cottage at last. Mr Roland went upstairs to change. Julian took off his macintosh and boots, and slipped into the sitting-room before Mr Roland came down from his bedroom.

Go to **244**.

After a moment's hesitation, Julian decided to go straight on. The countryside was very wintry-looking now. The sky was low and leaden, and he could see there was much more snow to come. He hurried on after Mr Roland, though he could see no sign of the tutor.

Down the lane and over the path that led across the common went the double row of footmarks. Julian stumbled on, his eyes glued to the footprints.

Go to **237**.

'Now, George, tell me what you were going to say about the Secret Way,' said Julian.

George explained that she had seen in the study: the eight wooden panels and the stone floor.

'It's odd, isn't it?' she said. 'Just what the directions said! I wonder if the entrance to the Secret Way is in this house, not in the farmhouse. After all, they both belonged to my family at one time, you know.'

'Golly, George! Suppose the entrance *was* here!' exclaimed Dick. 'Let's go straight down and look!'

'Oh yes, let's!' said George, her eyes gleaming.

'No,' said Julian. 'I think we should wait until everyone is in bed. It will be much safer. After all, supposing we ran into Uncle Quentin? I'd rather meet twenty lions than Uncle!'

If you think they go downstairs straight away, go to **248**. *If not, go to* **254**.

244

If you have arrived from **241**, *score* ◁ ◁.

'What's happened?' asked Dick and Anne, seeing that Julian was in a state of great excitement. But he couldn't tell them because just then Aunt Fanny came in to lay the tea. She was surprised to see Julian, until he explained that he'd had to turn back from his walk because of the snowstorm.

Much to Julian's disappointment, he couldn't say a word to the others all that evening, because one or other of the grown-ups was always in the room. Neither could he go up to see George.

'Is it still snowing, Aunt Fanny?' asked Anne.

Her aunt went to the front door and looked out. The snow was piled high against the step!

Go to **250**.

245

The four children crept downstairs through the dark and silent night. They made their way into the study. George softly closed the door and switched on the light.

The children stared at the eight panels over the mantelpiece. Yes – there were exactly eight, four in one row and four in the one above. Julian spread out the linen roll on the table and the children pored over it.

'The cross is in the middle of the second panel in the top row,' said Julian in a low voice. 'I'll try pressing it. Watch, all of you!'

Go to **252**.

246

After some hesitation, Julian turned left. The countryside was very wintry-looking now. The sky was low and leaden, and he could see there was much more snow to come. He stumbled on, keeping his eyes glued to the footmarks. It was tiring walking through the deep snow, and he could see no sign of Mr Roland.

Go to **249**.

Luckily the tutor didn't notice Julian. He went straight on and disappeared into the snow, which was now falling more thickly than ever. It was also beginning to get dark, and Julian, unable to see the path very clearly, hurried after Mr Roland, half afraid of being lost in the snowstorm.

Mr Roland came to the cottage gate at last, and

Julian watched him go into the house. He gave the tutor a little time to take off his things, then he went to the garden door. He took off his macintosh, changed his boots, and slipped into the sitting-room before Mr Roland came down from his bedroom.

Go to **244**.

248

'But all the grown-ups are in the sitting-room,' said George. 'I'm sure that I heard Father go in there just now.'

Julian hesitated.

'Oh come on, Julian!' said Dick. 'We're all longing to go and have a look!'

'All right, then,' said Julian. 'But we'll have to be very, very quiet.'

The two boys crept back to their room to get their slippers.

'Should we get dressed?' Dick asked Julian.

'No, you ass!' replied Julian. 'If we get caught and we've got our clothes on we'll have a far more difficult time explaining what we're doing.'

Go to **251**.

249

Then suddenly he caught sight of a figure up ahead! He hung back a bit because he didn't want to be seen, but the man plodded steadily on through the snow. Julian decided he could risk getting a little closer.

A moment later the man stopped suddenly. Julian stood frozen to the spot. The man pulled what looked like a handkerchief out of his pocket and, turning half around so that his back was to the driving snow, he blew his nose. As he turned, Julian could see that it wasn't Mr Roland after all. It was Mr Sanders!

Wearily, Julian retraced his steps to where the two sets of footprints had started, and this time followed the set of prints that went straight ahead. The snow had almost covered them by now, and they were difficult to see, but he could just make them out.

Go to **237**.

250

'Yes,' said Aunt Fanny when she came back, 'it really does look as if we're going to be snowed up. You poor children! You'll not be able to go out tomorrow the snow will be too thick!'

'Will Kirrin Farmhouse be snowed up too?' asked Mr Roland.

'Oh yes – worse than we shall be,' said Aunt Fanny. 'But they won't mind! They have plenty of food there.'

Julian wondered why Mr Roland had asked that

question. Was he afraid that his friends wouldn't be able to send those pages away by post or take them anywhere by bus or car? Julian felt certain that this was the reason for the question. How he longed to be able to talk over everything with the others. But he would have to wait until bedtime.

Go to **256**.

251

The two boys crept back along the passage to the girls' room.

'Now,' said Julian, 'I'll go first, and you others follow me in single file. And remember – no noise!'

Julian opened the bedroom door and listened hard, but all he could hear was the murmur of voices coming from the sitting-room. He stepped out on the landing, and at that moment Uncle Quentin came around the bend in the stairs!

'What are you doing outside the girls' room, Julian?' asked his uncle. 'I told you that you were not to visit George.'

'I wasn't visiting George, Uncle,' said Julian. 'Anne has run out of clean handkerchiefs, and I'm just taking her one of mine.'

'Well, hurry up, then,' said Uncle Quentin, and he went on down the landing to his bedroom.

Julian went back to the others.

'It's no good,' he whispered. 'Uncle Quentin's gone into his bedroom, and he's bound to hear us if we try to go downstairs. We'll have to forget about it for now.'

Go to **254**.

252

He went to the fireplace. The others followed him, their hearts beating fast with excitement. Julian stood on tiptoe and began to press hard in the middle of the second panel. Nothing happened.

'Press harder! Tap it!' said Dick.

'I daren't make too much noise,' said Julian, feeling all over the panel to see if there was any roughness that might tell of a hidden spring or lever.

Suddenly, under his hands, the panel slid silently back, just as the one had done in the hall at Kirrin Farmhouse! The children stared at the space behind, thrilled.

'It's not big enough to get into,' said George. 'It can't be the entrance to the Secret Way.'

Julian put his hand inside the opening and gave a low exclamation.

'There's a sort of handle here – with strong wire or something attached to it. I'll pull it and see what happens.'

He pulled – but he wasn't strong enough to move the handle that seemed to be embedded in the wall. Dick put his hand in, and the two boys pulled together.

'It's moving – it's giving way a bit,' panted Julian. 'Go on, Dick, pull hard!'

The handle suddenly came away from the wall, and behind it came thick wire, rusty and old. At the same time a curious grating noise came from below the hearth-rug in front of the fireplace, and Anne almost fell.

Go to **261**.

253

So George was right. The tutor *had* met them – and as Julian watched, Mr Roland handed over to Mr Thomas a doubled-up sheaf of papers.

'They look just like the pages from Uncle Quentin's book,' Julian said to himself. 'I say – this is mighty peculiar. It does begin to look like a plot – with Mr Roland at the centre of it!'

Mr Thomas put the papers into the pocket of his overcoat. The men muttered a few more words, which even Julian's sharp ears could not catch, and then they parted. The artists went off towards Kirrin Farmhouse and Mr Roland took the path back over the common. He was about to walk right past the gorse bush. Julian crouched down, desperately hoping the tutor wouldn't see him.

If you think Mr Roland sees Julian, go to **258**. *If you think he doesn't, go to* **247**.

254

If you have arrived from **251**, *score* ⤙ ⤙.

'Listen,' said George eagerly, 'why don't we wait until midnight and then creep down to the study when everyone is asleep to try our luck?'

'That's a good idea,' agreed Julian. 'Come on, Dick, back to bed! We'll meet here in George's room at midnight.'

The two boys went back to their room. Neither Julian, Dick nor George could sleep, but Anne went fast asleep and had to be awakened at midnight.

'Come on,' whispered Julian, shaking her. 'Don't you want to share in this adventure?'

Go to **245**.

255

'Oh do let's explore it now!' said George.

'All right,' said Julian eagerly. 'Anne, why don't you stay here and keep a lookout. If you hear anything – one of the grown-ups getting up or something like that – shout down the passage and we'll come back.'

Anne looked a bit worried. She didn't want to go down into the dark passage, but she didn't want any of the grown-ups to find her either! All the same, she nodded bravely.

One by one the other three lowered themselves into the dark hole in the floor.

Go to **263**.

256

'I'm tired!' said Julian at about eight o'clock. 'Let's go to bed.'

Dick and Anne stared at him in astonishment, but Julian winked quickly at them and they backed him up at once, yawning widely.

The children said goodnight to their aunt and Mr Roland and went upstairs.

'Undress quickly, put on dressing-gowns, and meet in George's room,' whispered Julian to the others.

In less than three minutes the children were sitting on George's bed. Julian told them everything as quickly as he could – all that George suspected – and how he had followed the tutor and what he had seen.

'They won't be able to get the papers away,' he finished by saying. 'The people at Kirrin Farmhouse will be prisoners for a few days if this snow goes on. If they want to hide the papers, they'll have to hide them in the farmhouse. If only we could get over there and hunt around!'

'Well, we can't,' said Dick. 'That's quite certain. We'd be up to our necks in snow!'

Go to **243**.

'Yes – I heard quite a lot of noise downstairs,' said Julian truthfully. 'But perhaps it's snow falling off the roof, landing with a *plop* on the ground. Do you think that's it?'

'I don't know,' said the tutor doubtfully. 'We'll go down and see.'

They went down, but of course there was nothing to be seen. They went back upstairs and Julian slipped into his room.

'Is it all right?' whispered Dick.

'Yes,' whispered Julian. 'Now go to sleep.'

Go to **269**.

'Julian!' said the tutor's voice suddenly. 'It *is* Julian, isn't it? I can hardly see you, the snow is so thick. What are you doing hiding in that bush?'

Julian stood up, rubbing his cold hands together. 'I wasn't hiding. Aunt Fanny sent me over to the farm to get some extra milk, because she thinks we may be snowed in and the milkman won't be able to get to us,' he said. 'But I caught my foot on a root or something, and fell over into this bush.'

Mr Roland looked hard at Julian as if he didn't believe what the boy had said.

Go to **262**.

Aunt Fanny was wading through the snow towards the kennel.

'It's all right, George. I can't bear that poor dog to be out here in the snow, so I'm going to take him in. I'm going to keep him in the kitchen, but you're not to come to see him.'

'Oh good – Timmy will be in the warmth!' said George with relief. 'Thanks awfully, Mother!'

She went indoors and told the others. They were very glad.

'And *I've* got a bit of news for *you*,' said Dick. 'Mr Roland is in bed with a bad cold, so there are to be no lessons today. Cheers!'

Go to **273**.

'Uncle Quentin will be working here tomorrow,' Anne reminded them.

'He said he was going to sweep the snow away from the front door in the morning,' said George. 'We could slip into the study then. It's Saturday. There may be no lessons.'

'All right,' said Julian reluctantly. 'I suppose we can wait until then. Oh I say – how are we going to shut the entrance up?'

'We can't leave the rug and carpet sagging over

that hole,' said Dick. 'Nor can we leave the panel open.'

'We'll see if we can get the stone back,' said Julian. He stood on tiptoe and felt about inside the panel. His hand closed on a kind of knob, set deep in a stone. He pulled it, and at once the handle slid back, pulled by the wire. At the same time the sunken stone glided to the surface of the floor again, making a slight grating sound as it did so.

Suddenly there was a noise in the bedroom above. The children stood still and listened.

'It's Mr Roland!' whispered Dick. 'Quick – slip upstairs before he comes down. I hope we all get back to our rooms without him seeing us!'

If you think they get safely back to their rooms, go to **270**.
If you think Mr Roland sees any of them, go to **274**.

261

'Julian! Something's moving under the rug!' said Anne, frightened. 'I felt it. Under the rug, quick!'

The handle couldn't be pulled out any further. The boys let go and looked down. To the right of the fireplace, under the rug, something had moved. There was no doubt of that. The rug sagged down instead of being flat and straight.

'A stone has moved in the floor,' said Julian, his voice shaking with excitement. 'This handle works a lever, which is attached to this wire. Quick – pull up the rug and roll back the carpet.'

With trembling hands the children pulled back the rug and the carpet – and then stood staring at a very strange thing. A big flat stone laid in the floor had slipped downwards, pulled in some manner by the wire attached to the handle hidden behind the panel! There was now a black space where the stone had been.

'Look at that!' said George in a thrilled whisper. 'The entrance to the Secret Way!'

'Let's go down!' said Julian.

'No!' said Anne, shivering at the thought of disappearing into the black hole.

Go to **267**.

262

Then suddenly the tutor smiled. 'Well,' he said, 'I do hope you didn't hurt yourself or scratch your hands on the gorse.'

'Oh no,' said Julian. 'I've got gloves on. I'm all right, thanks.'

'I don't think you'd better try to go any further,' said Mr Roland. 'The snow is getting heavier and heavier, and you may get lost. You had better walk home with me, and if necessary I can go over to the farm to get the milk tomorrow, if the snow has stopped.'

They started to walk back to Kirrin Cottage.

Go to **241**.

Dick, Julian and George made their way along the passage. It was dark and cold, and they had to feel their way along the walls. They hadn't gone very far when Julian stopped. 'Look,' he said. 'This is no good. It's much too dark down here to see anything, and none of us has a torch. We really will have to go back to the study and wait until tomorrow to explore properly.'

So they all turned back and were soon pulling themselves out of the hole in the study floor.

'We can't see a thing down there without torches,' George explained to Anne. 'Now, how are we going to shut the entrance up?'

'We'll see if we can get the stone back,' said Julian. He stood on tiptoe and felt about inside the panel. His hand closed on a kind of knob, set deep in a stone. He pulled it, and all at once the handle slid back, pulled by the wire. At the same time the sunken stone glided to the surface of the floor again, making a slight grating sound as it did so.

Suddenly there was a noise in the bedroom above. The children stood still and listened.

'It's Mr Roland!' whispered Dick. 'Quick, slip upstairs before he comes down. I hope we all get back to our rooms without him seeing us!'

If you think they get safely back to their rooms, go to **270**. *If you think Mr Roland sees any of them, go to* **274**.

Julian got under the bed just in time. The door opened, and Mr Roland's head appeared around it. George was pretending to be asleep, but she had her eyes open just a little. The tutor looked around the room quickly and then shut the door.

Anne was so tired that she had already gone back to sleep, but George lay awake, straining her ears to hear what Mr Roland was doing. She heard his footsteps go along the passage and down the stairs, then she heard the study door opening.

Go to **266**.

George walked around to the front of the kennel and peered in. Timmy was curled up, right at the back of the kennel, in a tight ball.

'Timmy!' called George.

Timmy jumped up and almost threw himself at George. He leapt at her and licked her face, then rolled over so that she could rub his stomach.

'Oh Timmy! I have missed you,' said George happily.

Just then George heard her mother's voice calling her: 'George! George! Come in at once.'

Go to **259**.

There was silence for a moment or two, then George heard the door of the study shutting and Mr Roland's footsteps coming back up the stairs. Then she heard the door of his bedroom opening and closing.

'Julian!' whispered George very softly. 'Are you all right?'

'Yes,' Julian whispered back. 'But I think I'd better stay here for a while longer or Mr Roland may hear me going back to my room.'

It was at least another half an hour before Julian wriggled out from under George's bed and crept along the passage to his room. He climbed thankfully into bed and was asleep in seconds.

Go to **269**.

Julian got down on his hands and knees and peered into the hole. He could just see that there was a space big enough to take a man, bending down.

'I expect there's a passage or something leading from here, under the house and out,' said Julian. 'Golly, I wonder where it leads to?'

'We simply must find out,' said George.

'Not now,' said Dick. 'It's dark and cold. I don't fancy going along along the Secret Way at midnight. Don't you think we should wait until tomorrow?'

Julian badly wanted to explore everything there and then.

*If you think they decide to explore the passage right away, go to **255**. If you think they decide to wait until tomorrow, go to **260**.*

268

They looked at one another in dismay.

'Now we'll never be able to explore the Secret Way!' wailed Anne.

'Don't be silly, Anne!' said George. 'It won't take long for Father to finish reading the paper, and then he'll go out and dig away the snow. You wait and see!'

Sure enough, about ten minutes later they heard the study door bang, and Uncle Quentin's voice calling to Aunt Fanny: 'Fanny! I'm going out to deal with the snow now. I'll be quite a long time, I expect.'

'Right!' said Julian. 'Now for the Secret Way!'

*Go to **276**.*

269

*If you have arrived from **266**, score ◁.*

When the children awoke next morning there was a completely white world outside. Snow covered everything and covered it deeply. Timmy's kennel could not be seen!

George gave a squeal when she saw how deep the snow was.

'Poor Timmy! I'm going to get him in. I don't care what anyone says! I won't let him be buried in the snow!'

She dressed and tore downstairs. She went out to the kennel, floundering knee deep in the snow. But Timmy didn't come dashing to meet her. Was he still in his kennel?

If you think Timmy is in his kennel, go to **265**. *If you think the kennel is empty, go to* **277**.

270

If you have arrived from **263**, *score* ⟳.

They switched out the light and opened the study door softly. Up the stairs they fled, as quietly as they could, their hearts thumping so loudly that it seemed as if everyone in the house must hear the beat.

The girls got safely to their room, and Dick was able to slip into his. But Julian saw the door of Mr Roland's room opening, so he dived quickly into the girls' room, which was nearest.

'Quick, Julian!' hissed George. 'Under my bed, in case he comes in to see if we're all asleep.'

Julian rolled under George's bed. The dust made him want to sneeze, and he held his nose hard.

Go to **264**.

Julian stuck his head around the study door to see if the room was empty, but there at the desk was Uncle Quentin! He wasn't working; he was just sitting reading the newspaper. Because he was holding the paper he didn't see Julian at the door.

Julian closed the door again softly and beckoned the others back to the sitting-room. Once they were all safely back inside, he said: 'Uncle's still in the study, reading the paper!'

Go to **268**.

272

They hadn't gone very much further when the passage suddenly widened out a little. Julian flashed his torch all around the walls.

'This is where this passage ends,' he said. 'Hello – what are all those things on the floor. They look like bottles.'

He shone the beam of his torch on to the floor. Sure enough, there were several old bottles, covered in dust and cobwebs.

'How do you suppose these got here?' asked Dick. 'I think they're brandy bottles, you know. They're rather the shape of that bottle that mother uses to put brandy in the Christmas cake at home.'

'I expect they were left here by smugglers,' said George calmly.

'Smugglers! Whatever do you mean, George?' exclaimed Dick.

Go to **275**.

273

If you have arrived from **259**, *score* ⌇.

'Golly, that *is* good news,' said George, cheering up tremendously. 'Timmy in the warm kitchen, and Mr Roland kept in bed. I do feel pleased!'

'We'll be able to explore the Secret Way safely now,' said Julian. 'Aunt Fanny is going to do something in the kitchen this morning, and Uncle is going to tackle the snow. I vote we say we'll do lessons by ourselves in the sitting-room and then, when everything is safe, we'll explore the Secret Way!'

'But why must we do lessons?' asked George in dismay.

'Because if we don't, silly, we'll have to help your father dig away the snow,' said Julian.

Go to **281**.

274

If you have arrived from **263**, *score* ⌇.

They switched out the light and opened the study door softly. Up the stairs they fled, as quietly as they could, their hearts thumping so loudly that it seemed as if everyone in the house must hear the beat.

The girls got safely to their rooms, and Dick was able to slip into his. But Julian was seen by Mr Roland as he came out of his room with a torch.

'What are you doing, Julian?' asked the tutor in surprise. 'Did you hear a noise downstairs? I thought I did.'

Go to **257**.

275

'There used to be quite a lot of smuggling around here,' said George. 'It was a long time ago – in the last century – but quite a lot of brandy was smuggled into this country from France. I expect the smugglers knew about the Secret Way then and used it to hide their cargoes.'

'How exciting!' said Anne, her eyes shining.

'It's obvious that this isn't the right passage,' said Dick. 'So we'll have to go back to the little room with the stone seat in it and try again. Come on!'

They retraced their steps down the passage and soon came back to the little room. They stood with their backs to the passage they had just explored.

'Now,' said George, 'do we go to the left or the right or straight on?'

If you think they turn left, go to **283**. *If you think they turn* *right, go to* **300**. *If you think they go straight on, go to* **292**.

276

If you have arrived from **268**, *score* ◠ ◠.

The coast was clear – the study was empty. Julian was soon pulling the handle behind the secret panel. George had already turned back the rug and the carpet. The stone slid downwards and sideways. The Secret Way was open!

'Come on!' said Julian. 'Hurry!'

He jumped down into the hole. Dick followed, then Anne, then George and Timmy. Julian pushed them all into the low, narrow passage. Then he looked up. Perhaps he had better pull the carpet and rug over the hole. It took him a few seconds to do it. Then he bent down and joined the others in the passage. They were going to explore the Secret Way at last!

Go to **284**.

277

A loud bark from the kitchen made her jump. Aunt Fanny knocked on the kitchen window.

'It's all right! I couldn't bear the poor dog to be out there in the snow, so I brought him in. I'm going to keep him in the kitchen, but you're not to come to see him.'

'Oh good – Timmy's in the warmth!' said George with great relief. She yelled to her mother: 'Thanks awfully! You *are* kind!'

She went indoors and told the others. They were very glad.

'And *I've* got a bit of news for *you*,' said Dick. 'Mr Roland is in bed with a bad cold, so there are to be no lessons today. Cheers!'

Go to **273**.

278

Julian and Dick both shone their torches on to the papers in George's hand while she tried to make out what was written on them.

Suddenly she began to laugh.

'Oh dear,' she said, 'these certainly aren't Father's missing pages!'

Julian took them from her and looked closely at them.

'Six pairs woollen stockings, 3 cotton vests, 4 shirts,' he read out. 'I know what this is! It's a laundry list, that's what!'

All the children laughed, though they felt disappointed that they hadn't found the missing pages.

'Well, come on,' said Julian. 'We mustn't hang around. This old trunk obviously isn't important. We'll just leave it here for now.'

On they went. Timmy ran up and down the line

of children, squeezing by them whenever he wanted to. He thought it was a very peculiar way to spend a morning!

As they came in sight of the room with the stone bench, George asked: 'Which way now? Shall we turn right or left or go straight on?'

If you think they should take the passage to the right, go to **297**. *If you think they should go to their left, go to* **292**. *If you think they should go straight on, go to* **300**.

279

Two bright beams of torchlight shone ahead of them, and the children saw that part of the roof had fallen in. Julian kicked at the pile of sandy soil with his foot.

'It's all right,' he said. 'We can force our way through easily. It's not much of a fall, and it's mostly sand.'

After some trampling and kicking, the roof-fall no longer blocked the way. There was now enough room for the children to climb over it. Julian shone his torch forwards and saw that the way was clear.

'The Secret Way is very wide here!' he said suddenly, flashing his torch around to show the others.

'It's been widened out to make a sort of little room,' said George. 'Look, there's a kind of bench at the back made out of rock. I believe it's a resting-place.'

They all sat down, glad for a moment or two's rest. Julian flashed his torch around the room again.

'Goodness!' he exclaimed. 'There are three passages leading out of this little room. The one on our right looks the straightest, but the one on our left is the widest. The one in the middle seems to have rather a low roof. I wonder which one we should choose.'

The children looked around them. Should they go right, left or straight on?

If you think they should go right, go to **292**. *If you think they should go left, go to* **297**. *If you think they should go straight on, go to* **283**.

280

'Let's try the left-hand fork,' said Anne. 'I have a feeling that it's going to be the one!'

The four children and Timmy set off along the left-hand passage. Just when they had all begun to think that they were never going to come to the end of it, they rounded a curve and there in front of them was a rocky wall. Set firmly into it were iron staples intended for footholds. These went up the wall, and when Julian turned his torch upwards the children saw that there was a square opening in the roof of the passage.

Go to **298**.

To his uncle's surprise, Julian suggested that the four children should do lessons by themselves in the sitting-room.

'Well, I thought you'd like to come to help dig away the snow,' said Uncle Quentin. 'But perhaps you had better get on with your work.'

The children sat themselves down as good as gold in the sitting-room, their books before them. They heard Mr Roland coughing in his bedroom. They heard their aunt go into the kitchen. They heard Timmy scratching at the kitchen door . . . then paws pattering down the passage . . . then a big, enquiring nose came around the door, and there was old Timmy, looking anxiously for his beloved mistress!

'Timmy!' squealed George, running to him. She flung her arms around his neck and hugged him.

'Listen!' said Julian. 'I think we'd better go to the study now and explore the Secret Way while everybody is busy.'

They left the sitting-room and went along to the study. Just as he opened the door Julian had a thought.

'I suppose your father *did* go out to dig the snow away, George?' he said. 'I hope the study is empty!'

If you think the study is empty, go to **276**. *If you think Uncle Quentin is in there, go to* **271**.

They were standing on the bottom step of a flight of wide, shallow steps that went out of sight around a curve.

'I'm going up to have a look,' said Julian. 'There seems to be a very strong cold draught coming down here. I bet there's an opening to the surface at the top of those steps!'

He set off up the steps and soon vanished around the curve. As he went on up he found that the steps became extremely narrow, and then all at once he saw light coming in above him. Looking up, he could see a smallish hole in the wall.

Climbing to the top step, he found that his head was on a level with the hole. He looked out. 'Why – there's Kirrin Farmhouse,' he said to himself.

Go to **294**.

If you have arrived from **275**, *score* ◁ ◁ ◁. *If you have arrived from* **300**, *score* ◁ ◁ ◁ ◁.

'Supposing we try the widest passage,' suggested Julian.

The others all agreed with him, so they set off down the wide passage. It was as low as the first bit of the Secret Way had been, under Kirrin Cottage, and they had to walk bent nearly double in places. Only Timmy was able to scamper along easily.

'Lucky Timmy,' said Anne. 'I almost feel like getting down on all fours myself. It would be easier!'

But before they had gone very much further the passage got a little wider and higher and they were able to walk upright.

Go to **289**.

284

Timmy ran ahead of the children, puzzled at their wanting to explore such a cold, dark place. Both Julian and Dick had torches, which threw broad beams before them.

There wasn't much to be seen. The Secret Way under the house was narrow and low, so that the children were forced to go in single file and to stoop almost double. It was a great relief to them when the passage became a little wider and higher.

Go to **288**.

285

They made their way back to the place where the passage divided and went down the left-hand fork. Just when they had all begun to think that they were never going to come to the end of the passage, they rounded a curve and there at the end was a rocky wall. Set firmly into it were iron staples intended for footholds. These went up the wall, and when Julian turned his torch upwards the children saw that there was a square opening in the roof of the passage.

Go to **298**.

286

'This is thrilling,' Julian went on. 'If George is right, and this Secret Way comes out at Kirrin Farmhouse somewhere, we'll somehow hunt through those men's rooms and find the papers.'

'You said that searching people's rooms was a shocking thing to do!' said George.

'Well, I didn't know then all I know now,' said Julian. 'We're doing this for your father – and maybe for our country too, if his secret formula is valuable. We've got to set our wits to work now, to outwit dangerous enemies.'

They walked on. The Secret Way just seemed to go on and on, and Anne began to wonder if they were ever going to get to the end! Quite suddenly Julian stopped. 'Look!' he said. 'The passage forks here. *Now* which way do we go, I wonder?'

If you think they should take the right fork, go to **291**. *If you think they should take the left fork, go to* **280**.

287

Taking hold of the handle of the door, he tried once again, turning it both ways. But still it refused to budge. Then he tried pulling it again. This time it began to open, very slowly and stiffly. It made a terrible noise, too, as the bottom of the door rasped across the stone ledge. Julian squeezed around it and then stood still, shining the beam of his torch around him.

He was in what looked like a small cupboard. There were rough stone shelves on two sides, and in front of him was another door. Stepping forward, Julian opened the door a crack and peered out.

Go to **293**.

288

'Have you any idea where the Secret Way is going?' Dick asked Julian. 'I mean – is it going towards the sea or away from it?'

'Oh not towards the sea!' said Julian, who had a very good sense of direction. 'As far as I can make out the passage is going towards the common. Look at the walls – they're rather sandy in places, and we know the common has sandy soil. I hope we shan't find that the passage has fallen in anywhere.'

They went on and on. The Secret Way was very straight, though occasionally it wound around a rocky part in a curve.

'Hello!' said Julian. 'Look here – the passage *has* fallen in!'

Go to **279**.

Dick was in the lead, shining his torch ahead of him. Suddenly he stopped. 'I think we've come to the end of this passage,' he said.

Julian edged past the two girls and shone his torch on the wall in front of them.

'I don't think this is the end of the passage,' he said after looking at the wall for a moment or two. 'I think this is a fall of earth. There are a lot of stones all piled up at the bottom and somehow it doesn't look as solid as the other walls.'

He gave the wall a thump with his fist, and some of the earth showered down on to the floor.

'Yes,' he said, 'I was right. This is just an

earth-fall, not the end of the passage. Now – how are we going to get past it?'

Go to **295**.

290

Above him was a stone wall. On either side of him was stone, but when he shone his torch in front of him he got a surprise. There was no stone wall in front of him, but a big wooden door made of black oak. A handle was set about waist height. Turning to look over his shoulder, Julian saw that behind him there was another door, looking exactly the same. Which one should he open first, the one in front of him or the one behind him?

If you think he should open the door in front of him, go to **296**. *If you think he should open the door behind him, go to* **302**.

291

After a little hesitation they decided to explore the right-hand tunnel first. Though it started quite wide and high, it got lower and lower as it went on, and the children once more had to walk nearly bent double. Then the passage started to slope upwards. Gradually the children became aware that cold air was getting into the passage from somewhere, though they couldn't see any light coming in. The fresh air was a great relief after the stale and musty air of the tunnel.

'Goodness!' said George, who was in the lead. 'The passage seems to be going up steps now!'

Julian moved up beside George and shone his torch in front of them both.

Go to **282**.

292

If you have arrived from **275**, *score* ◁ ◁ ◁. *If you have arrived from* **278** *or* **300**, *score* ◁ ◁ ◁ ◁.

'Well,' said Julian, 'I vote we try the straightest passage.'

The others agreed, so they all went on again, down the straight passage.

They hadn't gone very far when George suddenly had an idea. 'Julian – do you think the passage could come out at Kirrin Farmhouse?' she asked. 'You know what Mrs Sanders said – that there was a secret passage leading from the farmhouse somewhere. Well, this may be the one – and it leads to Kirrin Cottage!'

'George, I believe you're right,' said Julian. 'After all, the two houses both used to belong to your family years ago!'

'I say!' squealed Anne in a high, excited voice. 'I've thought of something too!'

'What?' asked everyone.

'Well – if those two artists have got Uncle's

papers, we may be able to get them away before the men can send them off by post or take them away themselves!' squeaked Anne. 'They're prisoners at the farmhouse because of the snow, just as we were at the cottage.'

'Anne! You're right!' said Julian.

Go to **286**.

293

The room in front of him was large and sunny, with a big double bed covered in a patchwork quilt and old-fashioned furniture made of some dark, heavy wood. Julian realised that this must be Mr and Mrs Sanders' bedroom.

'I certainly don't expect to find the missing papers in here,' he said to himself, shutting the door.

He squeezed himself past the door into the Secret Way again and stood for a moment on the ledge. He turned to look at the other door and wondered whether to go down and tell the others what he had found so far or whether to try the other door first.

Go to **296**.

294

Looking out of the hole he could see across a snow-covered field to the farmhouse. It looked very peaceful and snug, with a wisp of blue smoke floating up from one of its chimneys.

Poking his head as far out of the hole as he could, Julian realised that he was standing in the hollow trunk of a tree!

I suppose smugglers or people like that must have used it as a lookout to see if anyone was coming, he thought. How exciting!

He scrambled back down the steps to where the others were waiting.

'Where do the steps go?' asked Dick eagerly.

'Into a hollow tree,' said Julian. 'You can see Kirrin Farmhouse from a hole in the tree – it must have been used as a lookout by smugglers or someone. But we'll have to go back to the place where the passage forked and try again. I don't think the Secret Way can end in a hollow tree!'

Go to **285**.

295

The children all stared at the wall. It was obvious that without anything to dig with they wouldn't be able to get past the fall of earth. But they couldn't go back to Kirrin Cottage to find spades – it would take far too long, and, anyway, someone was bound to see them and want to know why they were taking spades into Uncle Quentin's study!

They tried scrabbling at the wall of earth with

their hands, but it was no good. The earth was too solid and tightly packed.

'I give up,' said Julian at last. 'We can't get through it. We'll just have to go back to the little room and try another passage. I just hope that this isn't the one that leads – well, wherever it leads!'

Go to **299**.

296

If you have arrived from **302**, *score* ⌒◁. *If you have arrived from* **293**, *score* ⌒◁ ⌒◁ ⌒◁ .

He decided to open the door in front of him. It opened towards him, over the ledge, and it was difficult to get around it without falling back into the hole. Julian managed to open it wide, squeezed around it without losing his footing, and stepped beyond it, expecting to find himself in a room.

But his hand felt more wood in front of him! He shone his torch and found that he was up against what looked like another door. Under his searching fingers it suddenly moved sideways and slid silently away!

And then Julian knew where he was! I'm in the cupboard at Kirrin Farmhouse – the one that has a false back! he thought. The Secret Way comes up behind it!

Go to **306**.

If you have arrived from **300**, *score* ◁ ◁ ◁. *If you have arrived from* **278**, *score* ◁ ◁ ◁ ◁.

'Well,' said Dick, shining his torch around, 'this wide passage over here looks nice and roomy. I vote we try this one. Come on!'

The four children and Timmy set off down the passage. It really was quite wide compared with the narrow, low passage from Kirrin Cottage, and the walls were sandy, like the walls in the other passage. It seemed to slope upwards slightly.

They hadn't gone very far when suddenly they felt cold air on their faces and saw a faint gleam of daylight. Looking up at the roof of the passage they could see the tangled, gnarled roots of a tree and a small hole where earth had fallen through on to the floor.

'Goodness,' said Anne, 'I can see a little bit of the sky. It's a lovely day. We seem to have been down here so long that I feel as though it must be evening by now!'

Go to **272**.

If you have arrived from **285**, *score* ◁ ◁ ◁.

'We have to climb up this rocky wall now,' said Julian, 'go through that dark hole there, keep on climbing – and goodness knows where we'll come out! I'll go first. You wait here, everyone, and I'll come back and tell you what I've seen.'

Putting his torch between his teeth, Julian pulled himself up by the iron staples in the wall. He had to go up a good way before he came to a ledge. Stepping on to it, he flashed his torch around.

Go to **290**.

299

As they all started back the way they had come, George suddenly caught her toe on something and tripped. Dick was just behind her and managed to catch her.

'Are you all right?' he started to ask, then paused. He caught sight of something in the beam of his torch. He shone the torch down on the ground, at the side of the passage, and there was a small tin trunk!

'Hey, Julian! Anne! Come and look at this!' he called.

The other two came back. Dick got down on his knees and pulled the trunk away from the wall, then started to lift the lid. It was stiff and rusty, but at last it opened. Inside there was nothing but a sheaf of papers.

'Look!' said George, picking them up. 'Perhaps it's Father's missing pages!'

Go to **278**.

They set off in the direction they had chosen, but very soon they realised they were going the wrong way.

'Look,' said George, 'here's that roof-fall we climbed over. This is the way back to Kirrin Cottage!'

They turned around and went back down the passage. When they reached the little room they were again faced with three choices. Should they go right, left or straight ahead?

*If you think they should go right, go to **292**. If you think they should go left, go to **297**. If you think they should go straight on, go to **283**.*

301

*If you have arrived from **307**, score ◁.*

'Quick! Hunt around again while we've time,' whispered Julian. 'Don't make a noise.'

On tiptoe the children began a thorough hunt once more. How they searched! But they could find nothing.

Then they heard the voices of Mrs Sanders and the two artists outside the door.

'Have you by any chance locked either of these two doors, Mrs Sanders?' came Mr Wilton's voice. 'We've been having a bit of trouble with them.'

Once again the handles were turned, but nothing happened.

'Do you suppose anyone is in our rooms?' Mr Wilton asked Mrs Sanders.

She laughed. 'Well now, sir, who would be in your rooms? I don't understand – the locks of the doors must have slipped.'

At that moment Anne was lifting up a large vase to have a look underneath it. It was heavier than she thought and she had to let it down again suddenly. It struck the table-top with a crash! Everyone outside the door heard the noise. Mr Wilton banged on the door and rattled the handle.

'Who's there? Let us in or you'll be sorry! What are you doing in there?'

Go to **309**.

302

He decided to try the door behind him first. He turned around and grasped the door handle. He tried to turn it first one way, then the other, but it refused to budge. He tried again, but still nothing happened. Then he tugged as hard as he could, but still the door refused to open. Finally he pushed with all his strength, but the door remained obstinately closed.

'Well,' he said to himself, turning around to look at the other door, 'shall I keep trying or would it be better to try this door?'

If you think he decides to keep trying, go to **287**. *If you* *think he decides to try the other door, go to* **296**.

303

Then Anne pulled a wastepaper basket out from under the table. 'Look, Julian!' she said. 'There's a lot of pieces of paper in here. Do you think I should go through them?'

'Well,' said Julian, 'they might have put the papers in there, I suppose, simply because that would be the last place that anyone would look!'

Anne tipped the contents of the wastepaper basket on to the floor and began to search through them. Meanwhile, Julian kept looking around the room. They could hear Dick and George moving about in the other bedroom.

Then suddenly Anne gave a shout. 'Look, Julian!' She was holding up a piece of paper.

Go to **312**.

304

As soon as Anne was safely down, Dick whispered to George, who was waiting in the cupboard: 'Right, George! Your turn!'

George scrambled down the staples as fast as she could. They could all hear the men battering at the door, trying to get it open.

'Come on!' said Julian. 'We must get back along

the Secret Way as fast as we can. Turn your torch on, George!'

George realised at once that she hadn't got her torch!

'I've left my torch in the cupboard,' she said. 'I'll have to go back and get it.'

And before the others could stop her she had scrambled back up the staples. She found her torch on the floor of the cupboard, then stood for a moment listening to the men pounding on the door.

Go to **314**.

305

Not noticing that the cupboard went further back than usual, the two men began to hunt around the room.

George was in such a hurry to get down the staples that she caught her jersey on one of them. Timmy jumped up at the wall. He wanted George. Why was she up that dark hole? He threw back his head and gave such a loud and mournful howl that all the children jumped violently. Timmy howled again, and the weird sound echoed round and about in a strange manner.

The men in the bedroom above heard the extra ordinary noise, and stopped in amazement.

'Whatever's that?' said one.

'Sounds like a dog howling in the depths of the earth,' said the other.

'Funny!' said Mr Wilton. 'It seems to be coming from the direction of that cupboard.'

He went over to it and opened the door. Timmy chose that moment to give a specially mournful howl, and Mr Wilton jumped. He got into the cupboard and felt about at the back. The oak door there gave way beneath his hand, and he felt it open.

'Thomas! There's something odd here,' called Mr Wilton. 'Bring my torch off the table.'

The men shone the torch into the back of the cupboard.

'Look at that!' said Mr Thomas. 'There's a door here! Where does it lead to?'

'Come on – we must go down,' said Mr Wilton, shining the torch into the square black hole. 'This is where the thief went. He can't have got far. We'll have to go after him!'

Go to **308**.

306

Julian couldn't wait to tell the others. He stepped into the space behind the sliding back and slipped the door across. Then, without bothering to close the heavy old oak door, he climbed down the iron staples again to where the others were waiting.

'Julian! What a time you've been!' cried George. 'Quick! Tell us all about it!'

'It's terribly thrilling,' said Julian. 'Where do you suppose all this leads to? Into the cupboard at

Kirrin Farmhouse – the one that's got a false back!'

'Julian! We can hunt for those papers now!' said George eagerly. 'Was there anyone in the room?'

'I couldn't *hear* anyone,' said Julian. 'Now what I propose is this – we'll all go up and have a hunt around the artists' two rooms. We'll have to leave Timmy here, though. He can't climb those iron staples.'

George didn't like the idea of leaving Timmy, but she gave him a quick pat and set off up the staples after the others.

Soon the children were on the narrow ledge.

Go to **310**.

307

The children got back into the wardrobe as fast as they could. The other three climbed back on to the stone ledge, while Julian stayed in the cupboard, listening.

He heard the two artists come into the room, and then he heard them rattling the door.

'It's certainly jammed, Thomas, and there's no key in it! I think we'd better go and find Mrs Sanders to see if she knows what's going on.'

Straining his ears, Julian heard a few words uttered in a low voice: 'Are the papers safe? Is anyone after them?'

'They're here in your room, aren't they?' asked Mr Thomas.

Julian gave a gasp. So the men *had* got the papers – and what was more they *were* in the room.

He listened as the two men left the room, then whispered to the others to come out. He told them what he had overheard.

Dick took the key of the bedroom door out of his pocket. 'I took this to make sure they couldn't unlock the door,' he said. 'Hang on. I'd better go and lock the door of the other room again.'

'What shall we do?' asked George.

Go to **301**.

308

Down in the Secret Way George had managed to untangle her jersey from the staples, and they all started to hurry down the dark passage. What a long way they had to go home! The children's hearts were beating painfully as they made haste, stumbling as they went.

Suddenly, behind them, they heard a shout. 'Look! There's a light ahead. That's the thief! Come on, we'll soon catch him!'

Go to **313**.

309

'Idiot, Anne!' hissed Dick. 'Now they'll break the door down!'

That was exactly what the two men intended to do! They began to put their shoulders to the door, and heaved hard. The door shook and creaked.

'Quick! We must go!' said Julian. 'Anne, Dick, George – get back in the cupboard quickly!'

The children raced for the clothes cupboard. Julian went first, then Dick, and between the two of them they helped Anne, who was not a good climber, down the iron staples. George was hidden among the clothes in the cupboard waiting her turn. She listened anxiously to the tremendous noises coming from the bedroom. Would she get down into the Secret Way before the men broke down the door?

If you think George gets into the Secret Way before the door is broken down, go to **304**. *If not, go to* **314**.

310

Julian slid back the sliding panel and stepped between the clothes. He felt for the outer cupboard door and pushed it slightly. It opened a little, and a shaft of daylight came into the cupboard.

There was no one there at all. That was good.

'Come on!' he whispered to the others. 'The room's empty!'

One by one the children crept out of the clothes cupboard and into the room.

'Look, Julian, there's a door between the two rooms,' said George suddenly. 'Two of us can go and hunt there and two here – and we can lock the doors that lead on to the landing, so that no one can come in and catch us!'

'Good idea!' said Julian. 'Anne and I will go into the next room, and you and Dick can search this one. Lock the door that opens on to the landing, Dick, and we'll leave the connecting door open so that we can whisper to one another.'

Go to **315**.

311

'Quick, back into the first bedroom!' whispered Julian.

They had just got the connecting door closed when they heard the door of the second bedroom burst open. Then they heard the voices of the two artists.

'Well, there isn't anyone in here, and nothing seems to have been disturbed,' said Mr Thomas. 'Let's have a look at the lock on your bedroom door from the inside, Wilton.'

'Good idea!' said Mr Wilton.

The children looked at each other in dismay. There was no lock on the connecting door.

'Into the cupboard and back into the Secret Way!' ordered Julian.

Go to **307**.

Julian studied the piece of paper his sister was holding up. 'But that just looks like a drawing, Anne,' said Julian.

'Yes, I know!' said Anne. 'It's a very bad drawing – like something a child would do. Those men aren't artists at all!'

Julian was pleased to have his suspicions confirmed, but they still hadn't found the missing pages. And search as they might, there was nothing to be found. It was bitterly disappointing.

'We can't go without finding them,' said Julian in desperation. 'It was such a bit of luck to get here like this, down the Secret Way and right into the bedrooms! We simply *must* find those papers!'

'I say!' said Dick. 'I can hear voices! Listen!'

All four children listened. Yes, there were men's voices – just outside the bedroom doors!

Go to **325**.

'Hurry, Anne, hurry!' shouted Dick, who was behind her.

Poor Anne was finding it very difficult to get along quickly. Pulled by Julian and pushed by Dick, she almost fell two or three times. Her breath came in loud gasps, and she felt as if she would burst.

'Let me have a rest!' she panted. But there was

no time for that, with the two men hurrying after them! Then they came to the piece that was widened out, where the rocky bench was.

'Now, which tunnel do we want?' said Julian. 'I can't remember!'

'Surely we go straight on,' said Dick breathlessly.

'No, no – we turn right,' gasped Anne.

'It's definitely left,' said George.

If you think they should go straight on, go to **318**. *If you think they should turn right, go to* **323**. *If you think they should turn left, go to* **329**.

314

If you have arrived from **304**, *score* ◯⌐.

As George stood in the cupboard her hands felt something rustly in the pocket of a coat she was standing against. It was a macintosh with big pockets. George's heart gave a leap. That was the only place the children hadn't looked – the pockets of the coats in the cupboard! With trembling fingers George felt in the pocket.

She drew out a sheaf of papers. It was dark in the cupboard, and she couldn't see if they were the ones she was hunting for or not – but how she hoped they were! She stuffed them up the front of her jersey and whispered to Dick: 'I'm coming down now!'

Go to **319**.

Quietly Julian and Anne slipped through the connecting door into the second room, which was also empty. Julian locked the door, and he heard Dick doing the same in the other room. Now they felt safe!

Anne set to work, and Julian began to hunt too. He started on the chest of drawers, which he thought would be a very likely place to hide things in. Dick and George searched hard in the other room. They looked in every drawer. They stripped the bed. They turned up rugs and carpets. They even put their hands up the big chimney!

There was simply nowhere that the children did not look. They even turned the pictures around to see if the papers had been stuck behind them.

Julian began to give up hope. Would they find anything?

If you think they find something, go to **303**. *If you think they don't, go to* **321**.

To the children's horror the torch-beam swung around to the mouth of the tunnel they were hiding in! Without a word they all took to their heels and ran as fast as they could down the tunnel.

Julian was very worried. If they were in the tunnel that led back to Kirrin Cottage, they would be all right, but if they were in one of the other tunnels, they would get caught, because both of them were dead ends!

Then quite suddenly, behind them, they heard a muffled exclamation and the sound of somebody tripping over.

Go to **327**.

317

Quick as a flash George moved over to the door and gave the key an extra twist.

The handle was turned and shaken again, then they heard the voice of Mr Wilton: 'It's no good. It won't open. Can the doors be locked?'

'It looks like it!' said Mr Thomas.

There was a pause, then the children distinctly heard a few words uttered in a low voice: 'Are the papers safe? Is anyone after them?'

'They're in your room, aren't they?' asked Mr Thomas.

The children looked at one another. So the men *had* got the papers – and what was more they *were* in the room!

Go to **301**.

318

They dashed down the tunnel, Timmy running ahead of them.

Suddenly Julian came to a halt and told the others to keep silent. He switched off his torch, George did the same, and they waited. Before long they saw the light of a torch cross the end of their tunnel, and heard voices.

Would the men come down the tunnel they were in or would they try another?

If you think the men come down their tunnel, go to **326**. *If you think they try another one, go to* **333**.

319

Crash! The door fell in with a terrific noise, and the two men leapt into the room. They looked around. The room was empty! But there was the broken vase. Someone must be there somewhere.

'Look in the cupboard!' said Mr Thomas.

George crept out of the clothes and on to the narrow ledge, beyond the place where the false back of the cupboard used to be. It was still hidden sideways in the wall. She climbed down the hole a few steps and then shut the oak door, which was now above her head. She hadn't enough strength to close it completely, but she hoped that now she was safe.

The men went to the cupboard and felt about in the clothes for anyone who might possibly be hiding there. Mr Wilton gave a loud cry: 'The papers have gone!'

Go to **305**.

320

*If you have arrived from **337**, score ◁. If you have arrived from **343**, score ◁ ◁.*

'We'd better turn back,' said George.

They retraced their steps to the end of the tunnel and eventually came out into the little room.

'Which way now?' asked Anne. 'Do we go left, right or straight on?'

*If you think they should go left, go to **323**. If you think they should go right, go to **329**. If you think they should go straight on, go to **328**.*

321

But search as they might, there was nothing to be found. It was bitterly disappointing.

'We can't go without finding them,' said Julian in desperation. 'It was such a bit of luck to get here like this, down the Secret Way and right into the bedrooms! We simply *must* find those papers!'

'I say!' said Dick. 'I can hear voices! Listen!'

All four children listened. Yes, there were men's voices – just outside the bedroom doors!

*Go to **325**.*

322

'Oh bother!' said George. 'Bother, bother, bother!'

'It's not as bad as all that,' said Julian. 'If you

remember, when we came to the place where all the passages meet, we needed to turn *right* to get to the farmhouse. So if we go back to the middle, we should turn *left*! I don't know why we didn't think of that earlier.'

'I just hope we don't meet the two artists on our way back,' said George.

They reached the place where the tunnels met without seeing the artists, but just as they started down the tunnel to Kirrin Cottage there was a flash of torchlight behind them.

'Come on!' said Julian. 'Run!'

Go to **329**.

323

They dashed down the tunnel, Timmy running ahead of them.

Suddenly Julian came to a halt and told the others to keep quiet. He switched off his torch, George did the same, and they waited. Before long they saw the light of a torch cross the end of their tunnel, and heard voices.

Would the men come down the tunnel they were in or try another?

If you think the men come down their tunnel, go to **316**. *If you think they try another one, go to* **330**.

324

If you have arrived from **327** *or* **336**, *score* ⌒.

'We'd better turn back,' said George.

They retraced their steps to the end of the tunnel and eventually came out into the little room.

'Which way now?' asked Anne. 'Do we go left, right or straight on?'

If you think they should go left, go to **328**. *If you think they should go right, go to* **318**. *If you think they should go straight on, go to* **329**.

325

If you have arrived from **312**, *score* ⌒.

'What shall we do?' whispered George. They were all standing by the connecting door between the two rooms.

'We'd better go down the Secret Way again,' said Julian.

'Oh no, we . . .' began George, when she heard the handle of the door of the first bedroom being turned. There was an angry exclamation, and then the children heard Mr Wilton's voice.

'Thomas! My door seems to have stuck. Do you mind if I come through your bedroom to see what's the matter with this handle?'

'Come right along!' came the voice of Mr Thomas. There was the sound of footsteps going to the outer door of the second room. Then there was the noise of a handle being turned and shaken.

'What's this?' said Mr Wilton in exasperation. 'This door won't open ... oh wait a minute, Thomas – I think I can get it open after all!'

The children looked at each other in horror. Would the lock hold?

If you think the lock holds, go to **317**. *If you think Mr Wilton is able to open the door, go to* **311**.

326

To the children's horror the torch-beam swung around to the mouth of the tunnel they were hiding in! Without a word they all took to their heels and ran as fast as they could down the tunnel.

Julian was very worried. If they were in the tunnel that led back to Kirrin Cottage, they would be all right, but if they were in one of the other tunnels, they would get caught, because both of them were dead ends!

Then quite suddenly, behind them, they heard a muffled exclamation and the sound of somebody tripping over.

Go to **337**.

327

'Listen!' hissed Julian.

'Thomas! Thomas! Where are you?' came Mr

Wilton's voice. 'I've tripped over a tin trunk or something and dropped the torch. We'll never catch the thief without it.'

They began to discuss whether or not to return to the farmhouse for another torch, and in a little while the children heard their footsteps retreating down the tunnel.

Julian counted to a hundred, then whispered to the others: 'Did you hear what he said about a tin trunk? That must mean we're in the wrong passage. The tunnel with a tin trunk in it comes to a dead end.'

Go to **324**.

328

They paused, uncertain which of the tunnels was the right one, but before any of them had time to stop and think sensibly about the way they wanted to go, they saw torchlight bobbing up the tunnel to their right.

Almost without thinking they started to run down one of the other tunnels. Timmy ran happily beside them. The tunnel went on and on, and the children began to think that they might have picked the right one when suddenly Dick, who was in front, gave a groan.

'Oh no!' he said. 'Look!'

And there in front of them was the row of iron staples. They had arrived back where they'd started from!

Go to **322**.

*If you have arrived from **320** or **324**, score* ⌒⌒⌒.
*If you have arrived from **322**, score* ⌒⌒⌒⌒⌒.

They hurried along the tunnel as fast as they could, but suddenly Anne caught her foot on a stone and fell heavily. She tried to get up, then began to cry. 'I've hurt my foot! I've twisted it! Oh Julian, it hurts me to walk!'

'Well, you've just *got* to come along,' said Julian, sorry for his sister but knowing that they would all be caught if they stayed there. 'Hurry as much as you can.'

But now it was impossible for Anne to go fast. She cried with pain as her foot hurt her, and hobbled along so slowly that Dick almost fell over her. Dick cast a look behind him and saw torchlight coming nearer and nearer. Whatever were they to do?

*Go to **335**.*

Julian slid down the tunnel as far as he dared, and strained his ears. He didn't want to get too close to the end of the tunnel in case the men shone their torch down it and he was caught in the beam.

'Come on, Wilton!' he heard Mr Thomas say. 'I think they went this way!'

Julian ran back to the others.

'They've gone into one of the other tunnels,' he whispered. 'Come on, we'd better get going!'

'But we don't know if we're in the right tunnel,' objected Dick. 'Should we go on or should we turn back?'

If you think they go on, go to **336**. *If you think they turn back, go to* **324**.

331

Timmy barked again. He was longing to get at the men. As the light of their torch shone around the bend George let Timmy go, and the big dog sprang joyfully to meet his enemies.

They suddenly saw him by the light of their torch, and he was a terrifying sight! His teeth were bared, and they glinted in the torchlight.

'If you move one step nearer I'll tell my dog to fly at you!' shouted George.

The two men hesitated.

'I don't like the look of that dog. Didn't Roland say he was vicious?' said Mr Wilton. 'Perhaps we should turn back.'

'That child isn't going to set her dog on us – she's bluffing,' said Mr Thomas. 'I think we should carry on.'

If you think the men carry on, go to **338**. *If you think they turn back, go to* **345**.

If you have arrived from **344**, *score* ◯⟋.

Dick took the sheaf of papers from under his jersey and gave them to George. She handed them to her father. 'Are these the missing pages?' she asked.

Her father fell on them as if they were worth more than a hundred times their weight in gold.

'Yes! Yes! They're the pages – all three of them! Thank goodness they're back. George, where did you get them?'

'It's a long story,' said George. 'You tell it all, Julian. I feel very tired!'

Julian told his uncle and aunt the whole story, leaving nothing out.

Go to **339**.

333

Julian slid down the tunnel as far as he dared, and strained his ears. He didn't want to get too close to the end of the tunnel in case the men shone their torch down it and he was caught in the beam.

'Come on, Wilton!' he heard Mr Thomas say. 'I think they went this way!'

Julian ran back to the others.

'They've gone into one of the other tunnels,' he whispered. 'Come on, we'd better get going!'

'But we don't know if we're in the right tunnel,'

objected Dick. 'Should we go on or should we turn back?'

*If you think they go on, go to **343**. If you think they turn back, go to **320**.*

334

The rug and carpet were still in place, just as Julian had left them. He turned them back, and then one by one the children pulled themselves up out of the hole. It was rather difficult for Anne, whose foot was still hurting her quite a bit, but with Julian pulling and Dick pushing they managed to get her up into the study.

Timmy had trouble getting out of the Secret Way too. George had to pick him up, which wasn't easy as he was a big, heavy dog. Julian lay on his stomach on the study floor and grabbed hold of Timmy as George lifted him. Together they managed to pull him out on to the floor, but poor Timmy didn't like it very much!

*Go to **344**.*

335

'I'll stay here with Timmy and keep them off,' said George suddenly. 'Here, take these papers, Dick. I believe they're the ones we want, but I'm not sure until we get a good light to see them. I found them in a pocket of one of the coats in the cupboard.'

'Golly!' said Dick. 'Well done!' And he sped off after the stumbling Anne. He told Julian what George was going to do.

'Good old George!' said Julian. 'She really is marvellous!'

Go to **340**.

336

They hurried on down the passage. All of a sudden George gave a yelp.

'Sh!' said Dick.

'But I've hurt my toe on something,' complained George. She shone her torch downwards, and saw at the side of the tunnel floor the old tin trunk that contained the laundry list.

'Oh dear,' said Julian. 'That means we've picked the wrong passage. This one leads to a dead end, remember?'

Go to **324**.

337

'Listen!' hissed Julian.

'Drat! I've dropped my torch,' they heard one of the men say. 'Oh here it is.'

'Come on,' said the other. 'The thief is getting away.'

'I don't think he went down here, anyway. We ought to go back the way we came.'

'No . . . no, you're wrong.'

They began to argue. After a while the children saw the torchlight fade away down the passage as the men went back. They sighed with relief. Julian counted to a hundred, then whispered to the others: 'What now? Do we go straight on or should we turn back?'

If you think they should go straight on, go to **343**. *If you think they should turn back, go to* **320**.

338

'She'll never set that dog on us,' said Mr Thomas. 'Come on!'

The two men started to run down the passage and turned around the bend where George was hiding. She tried to trip one of them up as he rushed past, by sticking out her foot, but he was too quick for her. They raced down the passage towards Kirrin Cottage.

But George certainly hadn't been bluffing when she'd said she would set Timmy on the two men. She stood up and shouted to Timmy: 'Go on, Timmy, catch them!'

Timmy flew after the two men, barking furiously.

Go to **342**.

339

Uncle Quentin looked a bit uncomfortable when Julian got to the bit about Timmy keeping the men off the escaping children.

'I was wrong to punish you and Timmy, George,' he said. 'I'm sorry about that.'

'It's all right,' said George. 'But don't you think Mr Roland should be punished? He deserves it!'

'He certainly does,' said her father. 'But he's in bed with a cold, don't forget. I hope he doesn't hear any of this or he may try to escape.'

'He can't,' said George. 'We're snowed up. But I think we should lock him in his room all the same. And I rather think the other two men will try to explore the Secret Way tonight, to get the papers back. Could we catch them when they arrive, do you think?'

'We'll put Timmy in the study tonight to give the two artists a good welcome if they arrive!' said Uncle Quentin. 'Let's have some lunch, and then I shall telephone the police.'

After lunch George went upstairs to lock Mr Roland's door. She thought she had better check that he was in the room, so she opened the door and stuck her head around it. But the bed was empty! Where was he?

If you think Mr Roland is in his room, go to **351**. *If not, go to* **347**.

340

George was crouching down, her hand on Timmy's collar, waiting.

'Now, Timmy!' she whispered. 'Bark your loudest. Now!'

Timmy had been growling up until now, but at George's command he opened his big mouth and barked. How he barked! He had a simply enormous voice, and the barks went echoing all down the dark and narrow passage. The hurrying men stopped.

'If you come around this bend, I'll set my dog on you!' cried George.

'It's a child shouting,' said one man. 'Only a child! Come on!'

Go to **331**.

Julian looked up.

A bright light gleamed down the hole. The rug and carpet, so carefully pulled over the hole by Julian, had been pulled back again, and now Uncle Quentin was there, and Aunt Fanny. When they saw the children's faces looking up at them, they were so astonished that they very nearly fell down the hole!

'What in the wide world are you children doing down there?' asked Uncle Quentin, helping them all out of the hole, with George pushing Timmy from below.

Aunt Fanny looked white and worried.

'I came into the study to do some dusting, and when I stood on that bit of the rug it gave way beneath me. When I pulled it up and turned back the carpet, I saw that hole – and the hole in the panelling, too! What *has* been happening – and where does that hole lead to?'

Go to **332**.

Timmy caught up easily with the men and grabbed one of them by the ankle. He fell over, and Timmy immediately took hold of the back of the man's jacket in his teeth and began to shake it furiously backwards and forwards.

'Help! Stop! Get this brute off me!' shrieked the man.

George came running up, almost too helpless with laughter to speak.

'I told you I'd set the dog on you,' she said. 'Let him go, Timmy!'

Timmy reluctantly did as he was told, looking up at George wistfully, as if he was wondering why she had spoiled such a very satisfactory game.

'Who are you?' asked the man on the ground.

'I'm not answering any of your questions,' said George. 'Go back to Kirrin Farmhouse or I'll set my dog on you again – and next time he'll do more damage.'

The two men turned and went back the way they had come.

Go to **350**.

343

'We'd better go straight on,' said George. 'If we go back we may bump into them!'

They turned the torches on again and set off down the tunnel. Suddenly they felt cold air on their faces, and saw daylight.

'Oh no,' muttered Julian. 'This is the passage that has the room with the bottles in it. Do you remember?'

A moment or two later the tunnel opened out, and there were the bottles.

'Oh bother,' said Dick. 'We chose the wrong passage.'

Go to **320**.

344

Once they were all safely back in the warm study they smiled at each other in triumph – they had got back what they hoped were Uncle Quentin's papers, and they had proved that George had been right about Mr Roland all along!

'I think I'd better go and find Uncle Quentin,' said Julian, 'and explain what's been happening!'

But just at that moment the study door opened and both Uncle Quentin and Aunt Fanny came into the room.

'What are you children doing in here?' asked Uncle Quentin, 'and what is that hole in the floor? What *has* been going on?'

Go to **332**.

345

One of the men took a step forward, and George saw him.

'Go for him, Timmy! Go for him!' she shouted.

Timmy leapt at the man's throat. He took him completely by surprise, and the man fell to the ground with a thud, trying to beat off the dog.

'Call off your dog or we'll hurt him!' said the second man.

'It's much more likely he'll hurt you!' said George, coming around the bend in the passage to enjoy the fun. 'Timmy, come off!'

'Who are you?' asked the man on the ground.

'I'm not answering any of your questions,' said George. 'Go back to Kirrin Farmhouse or I'll set my dog on you again – and next time he'll do more damage.'

The men turned and went back the way they had come.

Go to **350**.

346

Then Timmy gave another little bark, and George made up her mind. Sliding out of bed, she pulled on her dressing-gown and crept downstairs. She wasn't sure that Timmy was barking at the two artists, so she thought she would investigate before waking anyone else up.

She opened the study door and turned on the light. Timmy was sitting in the middle of the room, his head cocked to one side. As soon as he saw George he leapt towards her, wagging his tail. The entrance to the Secret Way was undisturbed and there was no one in the room. What had made him bark?

Go to **352**.

George went right into the room and looked around, but there was no sign of the tutor. She suddenly felt very worried. Supposing Mr Roland had heard all that they had been telling her father and mother? He might have tried to escape from Kirrin Cottage, snow or no snow, and warn the two artists at the farmhouse! If they got away, they might never be caught and punished.

'Well, if he has got out of the house, the only way he could have done it is by jumping out of the window,' George said to herself. 'The snow's pretty thick, and it would have broken his fall.'

She opened the window and looked down at the ground. There was nothing to be seen but clean, unmarked snow. There were no footprints.

He certainly didn't go that way! George thought.

Just then she was startled by a noise behind her.

Go to **353**.

If you have arrived from **352**, *score* ⟳

A fine sight met their eyes! Mr Wilton and Mr Thomas were crouching behind the sofa, terrified of Timmy, who was barking for all he was worth!

'Good evening, Mr Thomas! Good evening, Mr

Wilton,' said George politely. 'Have you come to see our tutor, Mr Roland?'

'So this is where he works!' said Mr Wilton. 'Was it you in the passage today?'

'Yes – and my cousins,' said George. 'Have you come to look for the papers you stole from my father?'

The two men were silent. They knew they were caught.

'Shall we take these men to Mr Roland, Uncle?' asked Julian, winking at George. 'Although it's the middle of the night, I'm sure he'd love to see them.'

'Yes,' said his uncle. 'Take them up. Timmy, you go too.'

Go to **355**.

If you have arrived from **353**, *score* ⌒⊋.

The children were all very tired indeed when bedtime came. Timmy was put in the study, because everyone thought that the two artists were bound to come back down the Secret Way that night to try to get the papers back; Timmy would certainly bark if he saw them.

George hadn't been asleep for very long when suddenly she was woken by Timmy barking. But it was only a small, rather quiet bark – not the really enormous noise that she thought he would make if the two artists appeared. She lay in bed for a moment or two, wondering whether she should go downstairs or not.

If you think she goes downstairs, go to **346**. *If you think she stays in bed, go to* **354**.

If you have arrived from **342**, *score* ⌒⊋.

George waited until she could no longer see the light of their torch, then she hurried along the rest of the passage, Timmy running beside her. It didn't take her long to catch up with the others. She panted out what had happened, and even poor Anne chuckled in delight when she heard how Timmy had flung Mr Wilton on the ground.

'Here we are,' said Julian as the passage came to a stop below the hole in the study floor. 'Now – I wonder if anyone has been in the study and noticed anything strange?'

'Is the carpet still in place over the hole?' asked Dick.

*If you think the carpet is still in place, go to **334**. If not, go to **341**.*

351

George opened the door wider and looked around the room. Mr Roland was standing by the window, staring out at the snowy landscape. He turned around as he heard the door open.

'Mother sent me to ask you if you'd like a cup of coffee,' said George. Her mother had done no such thing, but she didn't want the tutor to think there was anything odd about her coming into his room.

'No, thank you,' said Mr Roland, getting back into bed. 'Close the door behind you, please, Georgina.'

George shut the door and then locked it, grinning to herself.

Later on that afternoon Mr Roland decided to get up but, as the door was locked, he found that he couldn't leave the room. Though he shouted for help, nobody took any notice. And there he had to stay.

*Go to **349**.*

George wondered whether to go down into the Secret Way and see if there was anyone down there, but then she realised that she had no torch so she wouldn't be able to see anything. And anyway, she thought that she'd had enough of the Secret Way for one day!

Suddenly she heard a sliding sound followed by a dull thump. Then she knew what Timmy had heard. It was the snow, sliding off the roof on to the ground! She turned out the study light and went back upstairs to bed and to sleep.

But some hours later the whole house was woken by the sound of Timmy barking at the top of his voice. They all hurried down to the study.

Go to **348**.

It was Mr Roland, in his dressing-gown and slippers, with a book in his hand.

'What are you doing in my room, Georgina?' he asked. 'And why have you got the window open? You know that I've got a cold. Do you want me to catch pneumonia?'

'Yes,' said George under her breath. Then she smiled at the tutor. 'I was just coming to see that you were all right,' she said. 'Mother said I was to ask you if you wanted a cup of coffee.'

'No, thank you,' said Mr Roland. 'I had a drink of water just now while I was fetching my book.'

George watched as he got back into bed, then she went out of the room, closing the door and locking it.

Later on, when Mr Roland tried to leave his room, he found the door was locked. He shouted for help, but no one took any notice. And there he had to stay.

Go to **349**.

354

As she lay there, trying to decide what to do, she suddenly heard a sliding noise followed by a soft, dull thud. She chuckled quietly. Now she knew what Timmy had been barking at. The snow was sliding off the roof of the house!

She turned over and went back to sleep, worn out after the excitement of the day. Some hours later the whole house was woken by the sound of Timmy barking at the top of his voice!

They all hurried down to the study.

Go to **348**.

355

The men followed Julian upstairs, Timmy growling at their heels. George followed them, grinning.

She handed Julian the key, and he unlocked Mr Roland's door. The men went in and Julian switched on the light. Mr Roland was wide awake. He gave an exclamation of complete amazement at the sight of his friends.

Before they had time to say a word Julian locked the door again and threw the key to George.

'A nice little bag of prisoners,' he said. 'Now let's all go back to bed. I'm exhausted!'

The next day the police arrived, using Mr Sanders' tractor to get through the snow. The children watched as Mr Roland and the two artists were taken away in handcuffs.

'No more lessons these hols!' said Anne gleefully.

'It'll seem quite dull, now that the mystery has been solved,' said Dick. 'I hope it won't be long before our next adventure.'

Will the Famous Five have more adventures together?
Yes, of course they will! And perhaps YOU will be there again, too.

How many red herrings have you collected?

0–25	Very good indeed! The Famous Five must have been glad to have you with them.
26–50	Promising. Perhaps your next adventure with The Famous Five will be even more successful.
51–75	You took a long time getting there, didn't you? You'll have to do better than that to keep up with The Famous Five!
More than 75	Oh dear! Perhaps you should go back to the beginning of the story and try again.

Join the Famous Five on more of their exciting adventures in *The Famous Five and You*.